Little Known Tales
from Oregon History

A Collection of 32 Stories from
Cascades East Magazine

VOLUME II

FRONT COVER: (Top) A modern day wagon train fords the John Day River while following the Oregon Trail on its route from Philadelphia during the American Bicentennial. Photo courtesy of the Oregon Dept. of Transportation. (Left) Prominent Prineville citizens near the turn of the century. (Right) Prineville's first train "The Galloping Goose." Photos courtesy of the Crook County Historical Society.

BACK COVER: (Top Left) General Oliver Otis Howard, commander of the Department of the Columbias, gave chase to Chief Joseph and caused his capture. (Top Right) Meeting of an evangelist group. Photos courtesy of the Oregon Historical Society. (Center) The old Heisler stage stop. Photo courtesy of the Crook County Historical Society. (Bottom) A traveling salvation show near Hermiston. Photo courtesy of the Oregon Historical Society.

Published by
SUN PUBLISHING
716 N.E. 4th Street
Bend, Oregon 97701

Geoff Hill - Publisher/Editor

Copyright © 1991

Library of Congress Catalog
Card Number 88-90788
ISBN 1-882084-00-4

Foreword

The collection of *Little Known Tales from Oregon History* that make up this second volume have been reprinted from the pages of Sun Publishing's *Cascades East* magazine. The stories in this book were originally published from 1982 to 1988.

The idea for a feature on history in each issue of *Cascades East* came from George W. Linn, the first editor of the magazine. He felt Oregon, and Central Oregon in particular, was rich in pioneer history that, for the most part, had never been shared in printed form. He was right.

There are stories of individuals, families, events, achievements, conflicts, and unsolved mysteries. Illustrated with over 100 pictures and drawings, *Little Known Tales from Oregon History*, Volume II, will keep the memories of the past alive for years to come.

Table of Contents

Acknowledgements

It would be easy to fill several pages about all the contributors to this book, if we were to go into detail, but let's use the pages to share more of their stories.

There are 32 stories, and over 100 photos and illustrations included in this volume, which is primarily the work of 26 different authors. We thank each and every one of them: Russ Baehr, Norman M. Barrett, David Braly, Don Burgderfer, Olive Colburn, Art Fee, Michael Forrest, Marjorie H. Gardner, David H. Grover, July A. Jolly, Dorothy Kliewer, Steve Knight, Joe Kraus, Diane Kulpinski, Janet Mandaville, Joanne McCubrey, Donna Meddish, Mike Mitchell, Harry Robie, Francis X. Sculley, John Simpson, Lisa Slater, Robert Joe Stout, Martha Stranahan, Wilma K. Thompson, Bob Woodward.

Little Known Tales
from Oregon History

Vol. II

Traveling Salvation Shows

Those Old Camp Meetings broke up the routine of many frontier settlers. They were a time for celebrations...from revivals to reunions.

By Robert Joe Stout

Alone on the platform, arms lifted high above his head, his barrel-like chest heaving and his round face streaked with sweat, the meeting leader flung hosannas to the Lord above. The makeshift choir beside the platform clapped in cadence to his shoutings. Twenty people hunched in the dust at his feet, a bearded old man unashamedly sobbing, two girls in matching gingham dresses quivering in excitement and fear, the town's hunchback grimacing and gargling in a holy language of tongues. A youngish woman with stringy hair and a tic under her left eye pumped at a monstrous accordion as the camp leader's two young assistants worked their way through the crowd that was overflowing from the ten rows of benches they had set up earlier that afternoon.

But not everyone who came to the meeting set up on the outskirts of the old Oregon Trail town of Huntington, Oregon came to be saved. Half-a-dozen teenagers wriggled under the canvas and, laughing and dodging high weeds, headed for the family wagons where they could pet without interference. Drinkers vacated the nearest saloon to watch the entertainment and several horseshoe pitching contests temporarily were suspended. Button and rag peddlers, an ice cream wagon, a patent remedy "doctor" and one or two pickpockets began to ply their professions along the fringe of the crowd.

Camp meeting day highlighted rural America's hot summers until well after the First World War. Many famous evangelists such as Orceneth Fisher and Alfred Brunson (as well as some clever charlatans) traveled hundreds of thousands of miles to deliver their messages. Religion blended with entertainment, gossip,

Evangelist spreads the "good word" to a large gathering. The Camp Meetings were also a social time...pot lucks, baseball games and reunions were usually a part of this festive occasion. Oregon Historical Society Photo

Little Known Tales from Oregon History

No. 26

barter and games as virtually every inhabitant from miles around poured into town for the event.

"Nothing compared with it," my father's old friend, Roy Howerton, claimed. An archaeology buff who taught high school in western Oregon until his death in 1944, Howerton spent several years in Huntington when he was a teenager. "Life was a lot of struggling then," he told my Dad. "Those who lived out in eastern Oregon didn't have much in the way of intellectual or emotional stimulus. The camp meetings were exciting. People got caught up in them and

really believed in them."

Some of them, Howerton remembered, were "ding-dong affairs, with real preachers and real music." These often began in the morning, with a sunrise service, and lasted throughout the day and well into the evening. Former Gilchrist resident Anna Ganyo recalls family descriptions of camp meetings. "People would start coming in the day before. They'd camp in their wagons, or stay with friends in spare rooms or barns. There'd be a lot of running around and renewing old acquaintances, comparing notes, telling stories,

getting meals ready, generally working up to the day ahead. It was really festive. And you knew something big was about to happen."

That something big often began with a trumpet call at dawn. Out poured the eager, the faithful and the curious — farmers and lumberjacks, dowdy housewives, merchants and their families, children, servants, itinerants and off-duty soldiers — to participate in exhortations and prayers. Orceneth Fisher, who came to the West Coast as early as 1855, described these early sessions as "ground breakers" or "kindling fires" designed to establish a mood of seriousness and expectation. The evangelist led his slowly assembling audience in hymns like "Am I a Soldier of the Cross?" and declaimed upon the evils of alcohol, abuse of the body and failure to keep the Sabbath.

After an hour or more of singing and admonitions, the initial gathering would break up, then the group would come together again after breakfast for a longer morning session. Late morning and early afternoon meetings followed, each featuring prayers, hymns, sermons

These large tents were pitched near Hermiston. They would accommodate a large congregation and provide shade from the hot summer sun, and keep them dry during summer thunderstorms. Oregon Historical Society Photo

and exhortations. (Between times, the faithful were urged to seek the Lord through prayer, sometimes in special "mourners tents" set up expressly for that purpose.)

"Each time the worshippers returned for a new round of prayers and admonitions, the tempo seemed to increase," Ramona Monge described a camp meeting in the magazine **Out West** at the turn of the century. "By the time that the evening session had begun, the enthusiasm was contagious. You could feel it rippling through every mind and heart and muscle."

The tempo of the music also increased. Singers often accompanied the better organized camp meeting evangelists; almost invariably they were blessed with resounding voices that literally could be heard for miles. Evangelical "helpers" sometimes were scattered through the congregation to "witness for the Lord" and to shout "Amens!" and encouragements but by evening time, in the campground surrounded by lanterns and candles, enough local people had caught the spirit to keep the intensity high without outside help.

In Huntington, Roy Howerton recalled, one evangelist led everyone in a martial "Onward Christian Soldiers"-type of march around the campground. Others urged potential converts to "hug and touch each other, to fill each other with the Fire of the Lord!" The evening climaxed with a call to Jesus. Sometimes entire congregations would troop to the makeshift altar and fall on their knees before the evangelist. A Universalist minister, Peter Cartwright, reported that one camp meeting ended with some of those in attendance "suffering intense agony, others as happy as clams at high water; some kept their seats, while others were hopping, skipping and jumping."

Depending upon the evangelist's eloquence, and the size and frenzy of the congregation, the camp meeting lasted until well into the night. Evangelist Fisher, who had been ordained by the Methodist Episcopal Church, South, maintained that the night after a camp meeting "was as quiet and religious as the Peace of Bethlehem" with all who had been converted snuggled safely and warmly in the bosom of Christ.

Some camp meetings lasted two or three days, but most of those organized in eastern Oregon between the Civil War and the First World War were one-day affairs. In the larger towns on the camp meeting circuit, the evangelists and their crews set up tents. (In later years, they even carried portable wooden bleachers,

but these usually were organized as "revivals" and were both more sophisticated and less likely to be the town's only entertainment.) Others merely were held outdoors, in a field, the city square, or an auction yard.

Camp meetings were more than religious events, however. Many of them took on verve and bustle otherwise reserved for county fairs. Peddlers appeared as if by magic. Local politicians sometimes used the intervals between religious sessions to campaign for office. Men traded horses, nails, tools and good advice. Old friends, isolated by distances or weather, met and exclaimed, "Heavens! I haven't seen you since last meeting day!" Horse racing was frowned upon, if not specifically prohibited, but according to old-timers around Pendleton and La Grande, baseball wasn't and spirited games often took place.

Ramona Monge in **Out West** compared camp meetings to "family picnics of the biggest size imaginable." Youngsters from the isolated areas flocked together to play tag, marbles, sight-see and wrestle. Many of them had no playmates other than brothers and sisters and they rushed into new-found companionships with the abandon of shipwreck survivors. Their faces flushed with excitement, they ran to and from the sermons. Many of them got caught up in the religious fervor and rushed to the altar with their parents. Others saw the revivalists as spirited entertainers that later, back home, could be emulated or mimicked.

During Oregon's frontier days, big families were commonplace, and teenaged girls often found themselves babysitting for younger brothers, sisters and cousins in nursery areas set apart from the main camp meeting area. Thus confined, they became the targets of apple cores, spitwads and pinches as their teenaged male counterparts sidled away from the services to create a little mayhem. Often, however, the boys also would be collared and put to work chasing dogs, pigs, skunks and mosquitoes from the revival area, Roy Howerton recalled.

However, no matter how widespread or diverting the picnic-like reunions became, the camp meeting was, at core, a religious gathering. The evangelist, or "circuit rider," pulled the strings. In the days before the Civil War, many of these revivalists were self-educated, homespun men with Hell-and-Brimstone manners and great power of voice, but relatively little training. By the turn of the century, however, a majority of circuit riders reflected both education and training, and they followed a pre-

planned route from one community to the next.

"When I see a man preach I like to see him act as if he were fighting bees," Abraham Lincoln once told a questioner. As he brought his revival to its crescendo, asking for witnesses and the saving of souls, the traveling revivalist would shout, weep, wave his hands, fall to the earth, leap from platform to platform, appearing "for all the world like a frenzied banshee inflicted with a spirit from beyond," to quote a **Harper's Weekly** description from 1877.

Part mass psychologist, part demogogue, the circuit rider often directly addressed the Devil himself, writhing and sweating as he locked horns in mortal combat. Eight hours of praying, exhorting and admonishing, of fighting with the Devil and excoriating sin, interspiced with cadenced martial hymns, brought the evangelist and his congregation together in a feeling of exhalted oneness.

Critics of camp meeting conversions, such as a **Harper's Monthly** correspondent in 1917, contend that frontier people often led lives which, for the overwhelming majority, was "a monotonous grind, an eternal contention with desires that are considered sinful if externalized in other than channels ordained by convention and guarded by the law." Lacking excitement, lacking means of emotional release, they found in camp meeting religion both an answer to pent-up frustrations and a sense of excitement, a new self-awareness and a new concept of their environment, qualities which evangelist Fisher deemed necessary for true religious conversion.

Most camp meetings broke up with an air of renewal — and also of loss. As the frontier families climbed back into their wagons, bidding good-bye to relatives and friends, many of whom they wouldn't see again until "next meetin' time," they nodded and asked each other, "Did you see the way Clare got the spirit?" and "That Maisie, she sure makes good apple pie!" Many straightened their shoulders with new resolves, both about themselves and their frontier lives. Others, less permanently affected, shrugged away the feelings and concepts that temporarily had mesmerized their minds and narrowed their focuses to the things they would have to do, once home, to continue to survive and — hopefully — to prosper.

But almost all of them, secretly or overtly, admitted the camp meeting had been a great occasion, a rewarding diversion, a welcome break in an often demanding routine.

Little Known Tales from Oregon History

No. 27

Where's Shorty?

By David Braly

About thirty years ago a bridge was being torn down in Central Oregon. A skeleton was found. The skeleton of a human. Word spread throughout the region: Shorty Davis had been found! But he hadn't. The skeleton had belonged to someone else.

Shorty Davis is said to have resembled a dwarf. He was short and very fat. His arms were strong but much too long.

He arrived in Central Oregon in 1881. That was a year before the creation of Crook County, which originally covered the entire area. When Crook was created, it fell under the control of a powerful gang of self-styled vigilantes. Many men were killed by them and a few other men simply disappeared. One of the men who vanished and who was never found was named Shorty Davis, but he was a different individual from the one who arrived in 1881.

No one knew where Shorty Davis came from. He just arrived in Prineville one day, where he said that his name was Elias Davis and that he was looking for work. Prineville was the only large community in Central Oregon, a tough and lively cowtown. Charley Long, Hank Vaughn and other desperadoes hung around there. If a man didn't want to talk about his past, that was his business. Davis never talked about his.

Davis found work on the Lyttle place, a sheep ranch in the Prineville area. He worked as a herder and Lyttle paid him at the end of each year in sheep. Davis was a good worker, saved the money that he made from his sheep and earned the respect of the community.

He began to buy land. He bought a homestead on Eagle Creek, sixteen miles southeast of Prineville, and made it the headquarters of his own

sheep ranch. He owned three quarter-sections of land but he could graze his flocks over a much larger amount of territory. By 1895, he was living in a good house, had cattle and other stock and was the sole proprietor of one of the best sheep ranches in Oregon.

A local historian who belonged to a pioneer Crook County family recalled of Davis: "He was a bachelor, lived alone, and was a likeable fellow, but nobody seemed to know anything about him."

During the many years that he lived in Crook County he left the area only twice.

Meanwhile, trouble was brewing. In 1896, Crook County cattlemen met near the hamlet of Paulina and organized a "sheep-shooting association." There was talk by these men — many of whom were former vigilantes — of running sheepmen out of the county and taking over their ranges. The talk continued for several years, the animosity between sheepmen and cattlemen grew but violence was slow to arrive.

Then, one day in the summer of 1900, neighbors of Shorty Davis heard the cows and calves bawling on his ranch. They went over to see if anything was wrong. Something was. The sheep and other livestock were there, same as always. Nothing was missing. Nothing, that is, except Shorty Davis, his horse and his saddle.

Men in the area launched a county-wide search. There were no clues for them to follow and it wasn't even known how long Davis had been gone.

Soon the word got around that Davis had been murdered. Cattlemen wanted his grazing lands, it was said, and a man was hired to kill him. A $3,000 reward was offered for the

recovery of Davis' body and the arrest of his murderer. But no one came forward to collect.

The estate was held in trust for one year while the state government advertised for the heirs of Elias Davis to come forward and make their claims. No heirs appeared. Davis' property was escheated.

Soon afterward, civil war erupted in Crook County. In just one year, more than 10,000 sheep were killed by the masked riders of the Sheep Shooting Association. Men were shot and lynched, barns and hay burned, until the entire region was one large scene of desolation. Gamblers and former vigilantes controlled Crook's notoriously dishonest county government, so there was no recourse to the law. Many people fled and the letters of those who remained are witness even now to the terror that gripped the region.

The range war was at its savage height when a message arrived from Portland for the Crook County district attorney. Oregon's great school lands frauds cases were being tried in federal court in Portland at the time. Senators and congressmen — including a congressman from Prineville — were on trial for implementing a scheme by which worthless tracts of private land were traded for valuable public land. And the message said that one of the witnesses in the cases had information about the disappearance of Shorty Davis.

Crook County deputy district attorney Well A. Bell rode to Portland and talked to the witness, Christian Feuerhelm. Feuerhelm told Bell that Davis had been murdered for a motive, that the killer had later regretted what he'd done and had told

Feuerhelm about it in detail. Feuerhelm said that the killer had also confessed to what he'd done with Davis' body: thrown it into an eighty-five foot well in the vicinity, and then dumped Davis' horse in on top of him.

Bell returned to Prineville several days later. He said that federal and local authorities had all the facts now and that they expected to recover the body soon.

County authorities went to a well near the Davis ranch. It had been dug twenty years earlier to a depth of sixty feet, then been abandoned because no water had been found. Now it was only thirty-five feet deep. Nature had been filling it in with stones and earth.

Searchers were lowered down, where they began digging. They dug six feet before they found any bones. These bones were too small for those of a man or horse, so they kept on digging, all the way to the bottom of the well. Nothing.

About five years before Davis vanished, a dog had fallen into the well. There was no way to get him out and so he was shot. His were the bones which had been found.

The first and only clue in the Davis mystery was false.

But that same year — perhaps attracted to the case by the newspaper publicity aroused by the search for Davis' body — a lawyer decided to investigate and try to discover who Davis was. The lawyer was A.J. Derby, who lived more than a hundred miles from Prineville at the Columbia River town of Hood River. He had no way of knowing it at the time, but his strange search would last years and cover thousands of miles.

Derby learned that during one of the two times Davis had left Crook County he'd gone to Portland to visit Harry Maverrichi. Maverrichi owned a restaurant near Twelfth and Morrison. Maverrichi told Derby that Davis had a friend in San Francisco named Saphos.

Derby also discovered that Davis wasn't a native-born American. He'd been naturalized as a U.S. citizen about the same time that he began acquiring land in Crook County. He had given his name as Elias Davis, his birthplace as Montenegro and declared that he was especially anxious to renounce all allegiance to the Sultan of the Ottoman Empire.

The lawyer knew that a man born in Montenegro wasn't likely to have had parents named Davis. But the naturalization papers gave Derby no clue as to what the little man's real name had been.

He decided that Davis' San Francisco friend might have more information. He was right.

John Saphos knew more about Shorty Davis than any other man. He had known him all his life and they had lived together before Davis went to Oregon.

According to Saphos, Davis was a Greek immigrant. Davis had changed his name and gone to Oregon, said Saphos, to escape from other Greeks. Davis had complained that they were always borrowing money from him and never repaying it. Saphos said that Davis' real name was Leonidas J. Douris.

Now Derby's search for the heirs of Shorty Davis turned to Asia. He contacted the American consul in Smyrna for help in tracking down the Douris family.

It took a long time, but finally they were located. Leonidas had five brothers in Greece, none of whom knew that their brother in America had managed to acquire any property. The brothers chose one of their number, Constantine, to make the long journey from Athens to New York to Hood River to lay claim to the Davis estate.

Derby took Constantine and Saphos to the court in Prineville in May 1907. He proved the relationship between Shorty Davis and the Douris brothers. The peculiar physical appearance of the man made it easy to prove that Shorty Davis and Leonidas J. Douris were one and the same. The court ruled that the heirs in Greece would get the money received by the state for the Davis property, less debts and court costs.

The Davis estate was valued at between $75,000 and $100,000. In 1907, in both Crook County, Oregon and Athens, Greece, such amounts of money were considered fortunes.

That was the last solid development in the Davis mystery.

No one knew what had happened to the fat little man. Because his horse was gone also, he might have just rode away and left everything he owned behind him. He might have been warned to leave that way or be killed. But that wasn't likely, and that wasn't what the people in Central Oregon believed. They believed that the cattlemen had killed him.

Not too many years ago a skull was found in Crook County. The sheriff sent it to the lab at one of the state universities. He asked if it could be the skull of Shorty Davis. The newspapers and the people in Central Oregon asked that same question.

No, it wasn't.

Eighty-two years after the mystery began, it is still unsolved. The case of Shorty Davis is still open.

There was talk by these men—many of whom were former vigilantes—of running sheepmen out of the county and taking over their ranges. The talk continued for several years. The animosity between sheepmen and cattlemen grew but violence was slow to arrive.

Little Known Tales from Oregon History

No. 28

Oregon's Strangest Baseball Game

By David Braly

Folks in Crook County, Oregon were mighty proud when the Davidson Park baseball field was built in Prineville. They claimed that it was the best ball park in the Oregon interior and "the equal of the famous grounds of the Multnomah Club of Portland." The park had covered bleachers which could accommodate 700 people. Wide, very green meadows dotted by large shade trees were visible from the stands, even though the field was surrounded by a tall wooden fence. The Prineville Commercial Club built the park in 1911 on land donated by the Oregon & Western Colonization Company. The Club wanted to launch the park in a spectacular way. Their desire led to a series of events which are remembered and discussed in Central Oregon even today — and to the strangest baseball game in the history of the Pacific Northwest.

"$1,000 for Baseball/Monster Fourth of July Celebration at Prineville, Or./July 3rd, 4th and 5th/Three Days of Baseball. Three days of Special Entertainment. Three Nights of Outdoor Dancing. Three Days of Music and Sport/Gorgeous Automobile Parade — Three Prizes — $1,000 Purse for Baseball — 1st, 2nd and 3rd Money Prizes/Open Air Barn Dance/Big Array of Street Sports and Contests. Music by the Prineville Brass Band. Closing with a Great Fun Making and Unique STREET FAIR AND FAKIRS' CARNIVAL/ $2,000 Will Be Expended to Make This the Greatest Event of the Kind in Central Oregon. Over 200 people required to carry out the details of entertainment. Committee of Entertainment will secure accommodations (sic) for all visitors at reasonable rates . . ." So ran the headlines across half the front page of the *Crook County Journal* of June 8, 1911. Not only across the page: down it. There was no story, only the headlines.

Much was planned for this "biggest three-day celebration ever attempted in the interior." Among other features, it was to include the first street carnival in Central Oregon history, boxing matches, a parade of automobiles with prizes for the three best-looking vehicles, the reproduction of the streets of Cairo on the grounds of the Commercial Club, an Indian village, a Japanese tea garden, "Ufty Gufty, the wild man, Alexander, the most remarkable dwarf in the world, the battle between the Merrimac and the Monitor, Little Egypt, the most sensational dancer in the world." Prineville residents were told that "Professor Blondo will make his famous slide for life from a high pinnacle," and to "look for the bearded woman." This was heady stuff for a small (pop. about 2,000) Central Oregon cow town.

But it was the baseball games which were to be the big attractions. Every team in the state was invited. Four teams actually did participate: the combined Redmond-Bend team, the combined Wamic-Warm Springs Indian Reservation team, the Silver Lake Giants (from the little town of Silver Lake far south of Prineville in Lake County) and the home Prineville team.

On the afternoon of Monday the third, the games began after the agent of the Oregon & Western Colonization Company tossed the

The players shown are: Dr. Spalding, Bob Zevely, Sam Ellis, Ed Morris, A.R. Bowman, Raw Brewster, Jess Tetherow, Jack Dobry, Lake Bechtell, Peg Balknap, Bub Estes, Elmer Zeek. Apparently the photograph was taken before Hal McCall, father of Ex-Governor Tom McCall and hero of the game, joined the team.

first baseball to the mayor of Prineville. The first game was between the Silver Lake and Redmond-Bend teams. Silver Lake took an early lead and whipped Redmond-Bend 11 to 5. Prineville and the Indians took the field next. Because of the darkness (the game started late), there were only seven innings. Prineville won, 17 to 1.

Tuesday, Independence Day, community leaders roused people from their beds early with an "anvil chorus" to attend the 31-car automobile parade and patriotic celebrations. Balloons, music and flags were everywhere. Miss Georgia Cleek was elected "goddess of liberty." Afternoon sports followed a band concert.

Meanwhile, a change had come over the Prineville ball players. They were angry, indignant. They had learned that the Silver Lake Giants weren't men from Silver Lake at all, but professional baseball players. They were the winged "M" men, Gus Schroeder's Multnomah team of Portland, and among them was "De Neffe, the invincible southpaw from Michigan."

As angry at the deception as the Prineville team were two men who'd just arrived in town from Massachusetts, Thomas Lawson and Hal McCall. Of this pair, Lawson was by far the more famous. He was the "Copper King of America," the Boston tycoon who had formed the Copper Trust, then coined the phrase "the system" in denouncing those within it who had defrauded the small investors. Lawson was a colorful, maverick speculator who had a love of sports and of fair play. The other fellow, McCall, was his son-in-law, a son of Massachusetts governor Samuel McCall, and future father of Oregon governor Tom McCall. Lawson had purchased a Crook County ranch for his daughter and son-in-law as a wedding gift (he loved the area and it was chic at that time for rich, young New Englanders to acquire Central Oregon ranches) and the two men were on their way there when they arrived in Prineville. Aside from young McCall's outrage at the deception practiced upon the other teams by Silver Lake, there are two other facts about him worth knowing: first, he was immediately recruited by the Prineville team; and second, he is remembered even today as the greatest second baseman who ever played ball for Harvard.

The Prineville players wanted a chance at the Portland men. Prineville had the best ball team in the interior at that time, so if it and Silver Lake beat out the competition to face each other in the final game, the result promised to be very, very interesting.

Prineville first had to beat the Redmond-Bend team. The two met that Independence Day. Prineville took a quick lead, 6-0, but Redmond-Bend soon evened the score. After Prineville players became accustomed to the sharp delivery of Redmond-Bend's pitcher, Prineville managed to pull ahead again and win the game 14 to 6.

At five o'clock the Portlanders took the field against the Indians and quickly racked up a 6-0 lead. Then "Tomp" Osborne, of the Montana league, took the mound to pitch for the Indians. The Portlanders were frustrated by Osborne's remarkable delivery, and the city boys were whipped by the reservation players, 7-6. Terribly embarrassed by this defeat, the Portlanders lodged a protest with the local baseball committee that Osborne's name had not been properly filed. The rules clearly stated that a full list of players had to be filed with the committee before the start of a game. Osborne's name was missing from the Indians' list. The committee declared the Indians' victory forfeit.

The last game of the day, between Redmond-Bend and the Indians, was won by the former, 12 to 10.

The Prineville and Portland players would face each other the following day. It was a confrontation that the Prineville boys were looking forward to.

On Wednesday afternoon the showdown came. Bets were handled by one of Prineville's most prominent residents, Doc Rosenberg, and they were brisk indeed. The poor doctor was trying to keep track of bets made in money, hay and livestock. Because McCall of Harvard had been added to the Prineville team, the odds favored the little cow town's players instead of the big city's. Of course, most of the people at the celebration were from Central and Eastern Oregon, not Portland, and some of the big money was being bet by Thomas Lawson.

The afternoon was bright, the stands jammed with hundreds of spectators (the largest baseball crowd in the history of the Oregon interior), and the Prineville team optimistic, but the Portlanders took a quick lead. They batted in one run after another while the Prineville boys fumbled and missed the balls. Usually the Prineville infield worked brilliantly, but not today. It seemed that the Portland boys could do nothing wrong that afternoon, and that the Prineville players could do nothing right. In the first inning Prineville player Lake Bechtell was hit while at bat, and later managed to steal home all the way from second after a wild pitch to

first. But that was the only run for Prineville during the first five innings of the game. The Portlanders led at the end of the fifth, 7 to 1.

With the cow town losing — with hope of victory nearly gone—Thomas Lawson bet $1,000 that Prineville would win the game. Even his son-in-law tried to talk him out of it. But Lawson, who had once broken the bank at Monte Carlo, would not withdraw the bet, and observed that with the odds now so heavily against the home team he'd win more money when Prineville defeated the Giants.

The sixth inning began, and suddenly Portland's best players turned inept. The Portland pitcher and infield players appeared lightheaded, weak and clumsy. Prineville rolled over them. In the terse reporting of a local newspaper: "Hamilton singled. Tetherow fanned. Bechtel singled to center, scoring Hamilton. Bechtel scored on a wild throw to third. Ellis flew out to center field, two runs. Prineville has closed the gap. The score is a tie, 7 to 7.

Neither team managed to score during the tense seventh and eighth innings.

The Portlanders were at bat at the top of the ninth. No runs.

Prineville came to bat. The crowd was on edge. For the little cow town, 'twas now or never.

Lake Bechtell was the key man. He was walked. Sam Ellis singled, and Bechtell ran to second, then to third, and Ellis stole second. Ray Brewster batted a single, and Lake Bechtell ran home. That was the only run for Prineville that inning. But it took only one.

Final score: Silver Lake (Portland) 7, Prineville 8.

Prineville celebrated the victory almost as enthusiastically — perhaps more enthusiastically — than it did Independence Day or its new stadium.

And Prineville residents didn't forget the victory. Nor did other Central Oregon residents. Perhaps in Portland the game was regarded as some freak accident that happened out in the desert interior, but in the interior itself the game was remembered, discussed and debated for decades.

And why did the Portland players suddenly become weak and clumsy? Well, they themselves claimed that it was Prineville's high altitude and poisonous water that did them in. But the real reason they suddenly behaved as they they were drunk was well known: they really were drunk. They'd started celebrating too soon, downing one glass of whiskey after another, and they paid for it physically while playing ball in the hot Central Oregon sun.

Sacajawea, Move Over

by Janet Mandaville

Marie Dorion of the Ioway Plains Indians came to Oregon under conditions most would deem harrowing. Yet she came. And she stayed. As part of an overland party in the employ of fur company giant John Jacob Astor, Marie headed from the Missouri River Basin to travel 3,500 miles to the mouth of the Columbia River. Calculations are difficult, but she was probably in her early twenties.

Wilson Price Hunt headed up the group 170 years ago. He hired a French-Indian guide and interpreter named Pierre Dorion. And Pierre brought, over Hunt's objections, his family: Marie and two small children. Hunt would have been even more adamantly opposed had he realized Marie would bear a third child enroute.

The group started from Missouri in the spring of 1811 and by fall had reached Snake River country. Dwindling supplies forced them to slaughter the expedition's horses one by one. It's reported that only one horse, that of the Dorions, remained by the time the group reached the mouth of the Burnt River. Perhaps Pierre was concerned for his wife's condition. Yet Marie apparently walked far more than she rode. Did she leave the steed for burdens and for her two small sons aged two and four? Then for a few days, she had to ride, sometimes 25 or 30 miles a day.

And soon, in the snowy December weather, the Dorions dropped off the trail to seek seclusion for the birth of Marie's third child near the present towns of North Powder and Haines in Oregon. A day later, the family headed out to catch up with the main party, across the Telocoset Divide and into the Grande Ronde Valley.

Nine days later, the newborn died.

Winter saw the party across the Blue Mountains and into Umatilla Indian territory. Springtime 1812 came and part of the group turned back to the Snake River territory. The Dorions, with others, forged on to Fort Astor at the mouth of the Columbia.

Months later, with John Reed and other trappers, the Dorions returned to the Snake River Valley. Marie cooked for the party and dressed the pelts of the hunters' prey.

About two years passed. Then unfriendly Indians attacked the Reed party's post near Vale, Oregon. How many of the group were actually at the post or in nearby hunting shelters is unclear. But it seems that Marie and her children were settled at a cabin site across the river, perhaps at a newly built post. According to traditions, Marie heard rumors of the impending strike and attempted to warn her husband at his hunting camp. She was three days too late. Pierre had already been killed.

A single man, seriously injured, survived. Marie put him upon her horse and set out, still with her children in tow, to return to her cabin and obtain food supplies to care for the victim.

But she feared further attacks at her cabin. And when the wounded trapper died, she buried him in the snow and continued to wander in the Blue Mountains of eastern Oregon during the cold winter weeks. She sought assistance for herself and her sons, now aged five and seven. At some point the horse disappeared, was stolen, or was consumed for food. Hungry, cold, and very frightened, Marie could no longer cope with moving both herself and the youngsters. The boys were left near Meacham Creek, high in the mountain passes, so that she could travel more quickly to find help.

She made her way to a camp of friendly Walla Walla Indians, stumbling, falling, often inching along treacherous trails on her hands and knees.

Her tale and her condition upon arrival at the Indian camp immediately sent members of the tribe to backtrail and rescue her sons. The mission was fortunately a success. Then within two weeks, Marie encountered another party from the original Hunt party and recounted her many adversities, and the deaths of the members of Reed's group.

Many details of Marie's journey from the plains to the western frontier and her life along the Columbia and Snake Rivers are missing. After 1814 her life story for a time becomes even more sketchy.

She did remain in the Walla Walla Valley and marry again. And she had a daughter in 1819. What happened to this marriage to a North West Fur Company employee is not really known. But many, many years later, in 1841, Willamette Valley folks to the west of the Cascades Range suddenly have a neighbor in their midst: Madame Dorion. At some point married for a third time, Marie had borne two more children, and yet continued to use her Dorion surname.

Her death on September 3, 1850 is recorded in the Gervais, Oregon St. Louis Church. Records estimate that Marie was 64 years old when she died. Her grave lies beneath the church.

Monuments, rivers, mountain peaks, lakes, sculptures, athletic facilities and parks feature the name of the renowned companion to the Lewis and Clark expedition, Sacajawea. By comparison, only spasmodic attention is paid the Ioway woman of the Astorian party.

But Marie Dorion's fortitude is equally deserving. Only a few years later than Sacajawea, Marie came westward. And here she stayed. Here she made her home.

A roadway sign near North Powder, Oregon depicts Marie as the "Madonna of the Oregon Trail." A substantial memorial exists in the Marie Dorion Historical Park with its commemorative spire; that site lies four miles south of the Washington-Oregon border at the junction of Walla Walla River and Couse Creek.

In 1971 the Milton-Freewater Herald published a small book entitled, *"Marie Dorion and the Trail of the Pioneers."* And American essayist, novelist, and historian Washington Irving (1783-1859) paid her tribute in his work on Astoria.

"We cannot but notice the wonderful patience, perseverance, and hardihood of the Indian woman, as exemplified in the conduct in the poor woman of Interpreter Dorion. She was now far advanced in her pregnancy, had two children to take care of: one four and the other two years of age. The latter she had frequently to carry on her back . . . yet she had borne all her hardships without a murmur and throughout this weary and painful journey had kept pace with the best of the pedestrians. Indeed on various occasions in the course of this enterprise, she displayed a force of character that won the respect and applause of the white men."

Perhaps even more importantly, she continued in her own self-respect, Mr. Irving; her achievements certainly deserve our applause even today.

Dr. John McLoughlin – Father of Oregon

No. 30

By Wilma K. Thompson

Of all the heroic figures of the early West United States, Dr. John McLoughlin was the most remarkable one. He was a leader, a benefactor and a Christian. He was within the charmed circle of our national heroes. Often he was called "White-Headed Eagle."

John McLoughlin was born October 19, 1784 in Parish La Riviere du Loup, about 120 miles south of Quebec, Canada. His father was from Ireland, and his mother was born in Canada, but she was of Scotch descent.

John grew from a healthy baby into a sturdy little boy. His father said, "Smiles and sayings are the Irish in him."

John's uncle was a doctor, and he taught John to be inspired and have a desire to become a doctor.

John spent some of his happy youthful days in Mount Murray, the home of his uncle. Quite often he took walks along the bank of the St. Lawrence River. He even heard a lot of information about the Hudson Bay Company that actually moved across the Rocky Mountains. That sounded very good to John.

In 1798 John made a decision for a 14-year-old to become a medical apprentice. He learned how to set broken bones and to bleed his patients, drawing off poisons.

About 1800 John, 16 years old, crossed the Atlantic to Scotland to enter the University of Edinburgh and to learn how to become a good doctor. His license to "Practice in Surgery and Pharmacy" was granted to him in 1803.

He was 19 years old, tall and strong, with piercing gray-blue eyes. He had a shock of sandy hair and a booming voice, too. He was 6'4" tall. When he came home from Scotland he went into the service of the Northwest Fur Company of Montreal. That company joined the Hudson Bay Company, and McLoughlin kept his same position. That was when he left Quebec for the far west.

He didn't take a job as a doctor. He signed a long, elegant contract, promising that for the next five years he would obey the country officers and go where they wanted him to go.

He went on a large canoe, paddled by voyagers going west. They rode on rivers and lakes, week after week. At last, on an island near the western shore of Lake Superior, they stopped. They went into the huge circle of Thunder Bay, surrounded by forests. Actually, John was working for Hudson Bay Company and was selling furs.

For the first few years with that company Dr. John McLoughlin was a physician at Fort Williams during the summer gatherings, but in winter he took charge of a smaller post. Although the North West Company occupied many distant forts, Dr. John's were nearby in beautiful wooded country. There he bought all kinds of furs, but beaver was most important to him because its soft underhairs could be removed and made into the finest felt of the world. Beaver hats were expensive, treasured, handed down from father to son.

Dr. John had married a Chippewa girl, probably in a typical fur trader's marriage certificate. Her name was Marguerite McKay and she was part of the Chippewas, also the daughter of a Swiss fur trader. She had been married before, but her first husband had died.

They (John, Marguerite, daughter Eloise, and son David) rode on a ship, then crossed the Rockies on horses and canoes. Dr. John had his 40th birthday when they reached the northern area of the Columbia River into Canada — today's British Columbia. It took three and a half months to get to Fort Vancouver, Washington.

Dr. McLoughlin made his headquarters at Fort Vancouver, located on the edge of the Columbia River, not far from the Willamette River.

The selling of furs and many other actions lasted quite a few years. When he first went to the Columbia, he and his friends and employees were attached to Indians. A Scotch Highlander came there and gave a lot of

> *Oregon City was the capital of the entire west! In 1824 McLoughlin became the chief actor in the drama of Oregon. In fact, he was the first governor in the west.*

The John McLoughlin house before it was relocated and turned into a visitors attraction. Walter Boychuk Photo

Oregon Historical Society Photos

The McLoughlin house as it stands today in Oregon City. Visitors from all over the United States have toured the house still displaying the furnishings of McLoughlin. Priscilla Knuth Photo

music outdoors. The Indians became very interested in that. Dr. McLoughlin did manage to tell them never to make war on the Hudson Bay Company or any other Americans. So the Indians really became interested in music, Americans and Dr. McLoughlin. They fought no more. Dr. McLoughlin had an American missionary, Jason Lee, to teach the Indians religion and farming.

A ship came from Boston in 1829. When it arrived a fever broke out among the Indians. In four years over 30,000 Indians died near Fort Vancouver.

Dr. McLoughlin continued to work for the company, but he also healed many sick men who lived near his company.

Fort Vancouver was located on the edge of the Columbia River, not far from the Willamette River. Inside the enclosure were the workshops and a two-story building where *Governor* McLoughlin lived.

Dr. McLoughlin was the administrator of the Hudson's Bay Company, west of the Rocky Mountains. He was well-known and very famous. He helped people who came to Vancouver and Oregon.

Finally he moved to Oregon City, Oregon. Oregon City was the capital of the entire west! In 1824 he became the chief actor in the drama of Oregon. In fact, he was the first governor in the west.

When Dr. McLoughlin moved to Oregon City he built a saw and grist mill, giving work to a host of emigrants. He was a most genial man and was very sociable. He treated his wife with a lot of kindness. One settler said, "We could have died when we came had it not been for Dr. McLoughlin. He gave us seed and clothing and the bread we ate."

Dr. McLoughlin filed papers for American citizenship. He was called the "Father of Oregon."

At age 73, he passed away. He was buried on the banks of the Willamette River. Quite a while after his death his old house was repaired, and it was moved from the edge of the Willamette up to a street on the hill where most of the people lived. That house is open to the public. It still has his furniture, and the employees working there show pictures and give people information about McLoughlin. People from all over the United States visit that house which is kept open for visitors.

The "Father of Oregon" is remembered very well. His reputation is historical and fascinating. Even his grave was put there, in back of that fascinating home.

John McLoughlin 1784-1857

Little Known Tales from Oregon History

Dr. William Keil, Willies father.

No. 31

The Most Unique Crossing on the Oregon Trail

By Art Fee

The most outstanding crossing ever made by a wagon train on the Oregon Trail was led by a hearse that contained the body of a dead man. It had a strange hallowed effect on the Indians, for not one shot was fired at the caravan, nor was it harrassed in any way and not one life was lost on the long trip. Historian Steward Holbrook in his book *"Far Corners"* states "Willie Keil's 2,000-mile trek was the most unique crossing in American History. He was dead and in his coffin before the team was harnessed. Yet no flanking rifleman ever awed the enemies of a column of pioneers half so well as Willie Keil and his hearse."

Willie's father was Dr. William Keil, noted leader and founder of the Christian Colonies of Bethel, Missouri and Aurora, Oregon. The colony of Bethel had outgrown it's boundaries, more land was needed and rather than buy high priced land in Missouri, the Doctor decided to start another colony on the West Coast, where he could get free land through the Donation Land Grant in Washington and Oregon. When the advance party returned with a glowing report, his 19-year-old son, Willie, was the most excited person in the colony, his enthusiasm spurred preparation for departure. May 23, 1855 was set for the day when 35 heavy wagons, 250 travellers and a large herd of livestock would leave. But malaria, the dreaded scourge of the frontier, struck —Willie Keil became delirious. He begged his father to let him lead the caravan as he promised but on May 19th Willie died. To Dr. Keil a promise was as sacred in death as it was in life.

The Doctor ordered a lead-lined casket made, which he filled with alcohol and placed his son's body in it. He then had the coffin strapped to a light wagon. When everything was in order, the Doctor blew a long blast on his silver trumpet and the carvan moved West, led by a light wagon bearing a black casket and guarded at all times by two men. Then it moved ahead of the long column like the Ark of the Covenant when the Israelites moved through the wilderness on their way to the Promised Land.

Not only did his caravan travel in safety from the Indians, it traveled with a special blessing. There was little loss of stock, no sickness and no fevers. The plagues of cholera and typhiod, that had devastated so many caravans, did not touch his. (In 1852, 6,000 people died of cholera on the Oregon Trail. Some historians claim there are 15 graves to every mile of the Oregon Trail.)

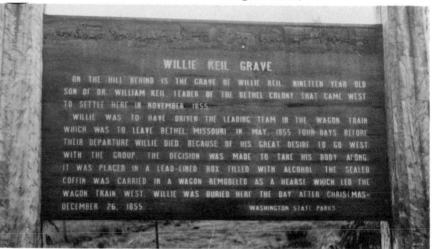

A historical marker on Washington Hiway six near Menlo, Washington.

The house built by Dr. Keil for his son August, at Aurora, Oregon. It is in excellent condition.

The well beside the house Dr. Keil built for his son August.

There is no question about the effect Willie's body had on the Indians. When the caravan was a short way out of Fort Laramie, it was stopped by a band of Indian warriors. They wanted to see what was in the black box. When the Doctor lifted the lid and they looked at the body of a dead man floating in a strange colorless liquid that kept it in a state of perfect preservation, they were terrified. Here was a medicine man who could preserve the dead.

Historian Russell Blankenship says, "Never was the hand of the red man raised against the men of Bethel. For years and years the Indians of Nebraska and Wyoming told with unflagging wonderment the story of the singing immigrant train which was led by a dead man."

The colonists were all outstanding musicians and music played an important part in their crossing. They carried a great array of instruments and sang and played about the camp fire at night and often on the long march. There were times when the whole cavalcade, including the loose stock, would be in step with the music. It shortened the miles, lifted their spirits and charmed the savage red man.

One day when the train was inching its way up the Platte River in Wyoming, the lead scout spotted a large band of Sioux warriors advancing. As the chief rode out from his armed men, a scout rode back to meet him, sending back word for the caravan to sing. Horns, stringed instruments and drums struck up a melody and 250 lusty voices broke into song. The caravan moved on to the beat of the drums and the voice of song.

Whether these Indians came in war or in peace no one will ever know. That day they stood motionless in the hot sun, watching a marvel they had never seen before and would never see again—a caravan of 250 singers, led by a dead man.

It was after leaving Wyoming that travel became extremely difficult. There was always the race against time; the Rockies were still ahead, and beyond them the Cascades. Keil did not dare to let winter reach the mountains before his caravan. There were also the mirages that danced ahead of the wagons, with beautiful blue lakes, only to vanish into hot burning sand. The wind blew, coating men's raw throats and tongues with dust, burning their eyes with alkali and grinding tempers raw. There were flash storms when lightening crashed and large hail stones came down in salvos. Most of the time the cruel sun beat down without mercy and there was no place to hide.

All along the way there was discarded furniture, a grim reminder that some family had parted with cherished heirlooms. There were the white bones of horses and cattle, broken and discarded wagons, and newly dug graves.

Worst of all were the scenes on Indian attack where all that remained were the twisted iron rims and steel braces of the burned wagons. Dead cattle and horses lay in grotesque shapes and the decaying bodies of the massacred victims lay unburied in the hot sun. Scenes like these can do strange things to any man's personality and especially to a leader who is responsible for the safety and welfare of 250 souls.

The worst part of the crossing was the desert west of Fort Hall. Here the Trail was literally mapped out by the graves and bones along the way. In places there were over a hundred carcasses to the mile. The heat was unbearable. The dust in places was knee deep. For miles there was neither grass nor water. Three and four head of stock died every day on this stretch, but they yoked and harnessed more of the loose stock and kept going. In spite of this, the Doctor kept up their moral by his positive attitude. He prophesied that all of the wagons would get through—and they did.

The Indians, who massacred other caravans, helped this one through. Dr. Keil treated the red men with kindness. He fed them when they were hungry, nursed them when they were sick, and they returned his favors. When his caravan missed the trail, two friendly Indians guided it back.

Other caravans were constantly

Continued on Page 29

Willie's grave.

The Old Hall at Pringle Flat

By Lisa Slater

Rising tall above the sagebrush,
on the high desert in Oregon,
stands a weatherbeaten structure:
the old hall at Pringle Flat.
The homesteaders would gather
for their socials and their dances,
while, among them danced a queen,
who caused all men's hearts to flutter,
all women's eyes to gleam.

From the gold rush days in Dawson,
where she made her claim to fame;
this darling of the sourdoughs,
in the days of '98;
worked a homestead claim near Brothers.
For years that numbered three,
she graced the hall with song,
lilting laughter, dancing feet.

Birds nest among the rafters now.
Wind whistles through the cracks,
whispering a lonely echo
of days long gone and past.
Yet, on one wall in letters bold,
a bit of history will unfold.
Written there by her own hand,
'KATE E. ROCKWELL, DEC. 25, 1914.'
Klondike Kate, the Yukon Queen!

You can still stand among the shambles,
and gaze at the writing on the wall.
Your heart might fill with sadness;
for this little bit of history
will barely cast a shadow.
They are saying back in Brothers;
the old hall is coming down.

NOTE: Between 1914 and 1917, Klondike Kate
worked a 320 acre homestead claim three miles
Northeast of Brothers, Oregon. The buildings
on her claim have long since been torn down.
As of this writing, the old hall at Pringle
Flat, Oregon is still standing.

Lisa Slater

Little Known Tales from Oregon History

No. 33

Mystery of the Ochocos

By Dorothy Kliewer

One of Oregon's unsolved mysteries came to light in 1930 during Franklin Roosevelt's administration when the Forestry Service sent a forest ranger into the pine timber of the Ochoco Mountains of Central Oregon to estimate the number of board feet in that largest of all pine forests in the United States. The ranger, who spent many days traipsing the forest walked through areas that few white men had ever seen. Only deer and elk hunters had ventured there in those days. In a clearing on the east slope he discovered a rotting lot with six horse skeletons tied to it. The skeletons were complete with saddles and bridles and it was obvious that whoever had left the horses there had meant to return. Why hadn't they?

Many ideas were advanced about the skeletons though it was generally believed that the horses had belonged to six masked men who, in 1863, rode into Canyon City, Oregon at dusk and stole all the gold from the miners' sluice boxes. They hid out that night, and the next day rode into Dayville where they stopped long enough to rob the bank.

A posse set out in hot pursuit though lost their trail in the Ochoco Mountains and obviously did not discover the six horses tied to a log. The masked bandits vanished as if swallowed by the earth and that may, in fact, be what really happened to them.

In those days people took excellent care of their horses and good saddles were expensive. No matter how bad a man was, he took adequate care of his horse and the bandits would have turned their animals loose if they hadn't meant to return. And if the robbers had changed horses there in Burglar's Flat, why didn't they take the saddles and turn the animals loose so they wouldn't starve?

No one in the nearby town of Prineville saw any masked men that day though strangers were a common sight. Six strangers together would have been noticed, however. Perhaps they split up or were even residents of that community, which would explain why the posse lost their trail. Gold is very heavy and the horses would have tired quickly carrying the amount of gold the bandits had stolen — $40,000 in gold brick from the bank and the dust from the sluices. Unless they changed horses or had a well-concealed hiding place, the posse would have overtaken horses winded from such a ride, but the posse continued on to Shaniko without finding a trace of the masked men.

The mystery of six horses left in a clearing near Stein's Pillar at a place now called Viewpoint has never really been solved though research of the area tells us that there was a gold mine near Viewpoint in those days called The Four Dutchman. It was owned by four California men who left it one summer and never returned. They'd had assays made of the gold they found there, so there is a record of the mine's existence. That mine shaft has never been discovered. Is it because the masked robbers took refuge in the mine shaft and it caved in on them? Is there a fortune in gold hidden in a caved-in mine shaft waiting to be discovered in the tall pine-covered slopes of the Ochoco Mountains?

Stein's Pillar is said to have been visible from the clearing where the skeletons of 6 horses tied to a log were found. A fortune in stolen gold bricks is thought to be in the area.   Ed Park Photo

Little Known Tales from Oregon History

No. 34

Oregon Trail – 1920's Style

By Marjorie H. Gardner

In 1851 my great-grandfather moved his family from Missouri to Oregon, settling near Eugene. In 1922 my father moved *his* family from Oregon to California. Why, I'll never know.

I was five, my brother, Paul, was two, and our party included our California grandparents who had driven up to scout the route and to shepherd us on the trip south.

We had an Overland, my grandparents, a Hupmobile, both open touring cars with imitation leather seats and flapping side curtains with cracked isinglass peepholes. The roads encountered were not all that much different, in some instances, from the ones Great-Grandfather had coaxed the oxen over some seventy years before.

It was August. The highway that became 99 was under construction. The many detours took us through farm yards and badlands, over corduroy roads, wagon ruts, and Indian trails. When we came to a river we had to wait for the ferry. This might delay us mere minutes, or up into the next day. But, back then, if you were in a car, delay was the name of the game.

Actually, the detours weren't much worse than the main road, in some stretches the old stagecoach road. At Wolf Creek Pass, teams of horses were on hand to tow the Model T's up the mountain. Our little caravan made it on its own, but the laboring teams ahead set our rate of speed.

Intermittent rains further slowed us down, as Papa had to stop often to get out and give the windshield a swipe of the rag kept for that purpose. The Hup, however, was equipped with a marvelous device. It was called a Wind Shield Wiper. When the windshield misted over all Grandpa had to do was reach up and push the scraper gadget from left to right. Then, when he had again been driving blind for awhile, he pushed it from *right* to *left*.

Worse than the rain, was the dust, raised by the road equipment and panting cars in front, which forced us to inch along squint-eyed. Unlike rain, dust never dried up, but settled on the automobiles, the travel gear, and on ourselves.

Veils and dusters had gone out of style but touring ladies still wore special outfits. These were khaki (dust color) for obvious reason and consisted of a high-necked, long-sleeved shirt, calf-length skirt, and matching hat. Grandma, who for some reason was a more classy dresser than Mama, wore a Divided Skirt. This affair buttoned down the front but could be worn unbuttoned, displaying what we today might describe as a very full pair of pants. In those days women never wore pants, so this had to be called a skirt. Flappers wore knickers and all women wore union suits, step-ins, bloomers, or teddies—the very cat's pajamas—but never pants or *panties*.

Flappers' boy friends wore breeches (mutton-legged above the knee, circulation stopper below), contained in leather puttees. Papa and Grandpa wore their second best trousers.

Pangs of hunger, as now, forced regular stops but in 1922 there was no McDonald's. The food for that entire trip rode with us in three grocery cartons. One box held tin plates, cutlery, skillet, and coffee pot, and the other two, cold cereal, canned milk, coffee, sugar, homemade bread, bacon, eggs, fresh and canned fruit. We feasted on meat loaf, fried chicken, ham, cake, and pie—the relatives had given us a fine send-off. We didn't know about refrigeration, remained blissfully unaware that before the journey was over some of those victuals should have landed us in the nearest hospital.

A blanket spread on the ground formed our table. The bare dirt made a good enough seat for Paul and me, while the grownups sat on the

This auto camp near Eugene was sprucer than some that we encountered.

Marjorie Gardner Photo

running boards, the most useful automotive accessory ever devised.

Just when we were, for a change, making pretty good time, there was sure to be a blowout or puncture, or one of the drivers thought it time to pull to a stop and poke a stick down the gas tank. If it came out dry we had to hunt up a refill.

Some towns boasted one of those newfangled blue and white service stations with the flagpole in front, making our mission easily accomplished. More often we had to ask around for the nearest tank wagon. Then, at some general store or feed store, we waited until the proprietor had time to wheel out the gasoline. At twenty-two to twenty-six cents a gallon, that trip cost a fortune. The following year the price dropped to a more reasonable eighteen cents.

Unless we'd had extra car trouble, the mileage racked up each day depended on the distance between auto camps—no Holiday Inn. Auto camps were usually found among groves of trees and should have provided oasis after the day's drive, during which we might have covered as much as 130 miles. Unfortunately, there was a drawback. With a few exceptions, the sanitary facilities bore no more resemblance to those of today's Interstate rest stops than a Stanley Steamer to the newest Cadillac. They were probably two-holers but we seldom checked. Get within twenty feet and we took to the woods.

With the Overland and Hup settled in camp spaces, Papa and Grandpa unrolled the tarp from the top of the Overland and pegged it down about six feet from the side wheels. This made a dandy bedroom for our parents. Paul and I slept in the front and back seats of the car. Grandpa and Grandma traveled in style—they had a *boughten* tent.

All four grownups spread their bedrolls on the army cots that rode behind the board clamped from fender to fender of the Overland and when it came time to setting them up the men began cussing. The cots unfolded easily enough, and the first brace went in okay, but getting that second one adjusted was worse than trying to park a Mack truck in a space designed for a roadster. Army cots had to be surplus from the American Revolution and the reason there were so many of them around was that no self-respecting soldier would use one. The hard ground was more comfortable—Valley Forge was more comfortable!

Another restless night, another rainy/dusty/muddy day. We chugged up the switchbacks north of Ashland and crossed the state line. California! The storied land Grandma had told us so much about. It looked just like the part of Oregon we had been seeing, but not nearly as nice as the Oregon we called home. Finally, after a total of six days' travel, we reached our new home south of San Francisco.

Three years later, I'm told, we made the trip in reverse, driving back to Oregon to visit the kin. We sped over the completed highway at thirty-five miles an hour and took only four days. We purchased fresh food supplies along the way and stayed the night at auto courts—tiny cottages with one or two rooms, besides the kitchen, bath, and a garage.

The mud, dust, and ferries were gone and the Overland had a brand new Wind Shield Wiper but, strangely enough, I don't remember that trip.

I don't even remember much about traveling that route last year. We could have had our choice of restaurants and motels, but we ate only one meal along the way and didn't stop for the night. Now, you see, the trip takes only one day.

BELOW: We didn't need picnic tables, but running boards never should have been phased out. This shows the Overland (with missing isinglass) and Hupmobile. I'm the kid in the washbowl hat.

Little Known Tales from Oregon History

Ka-Ton-Ka, Oregon's "Perfect Remedy"

By Harry Robie

The Oregon Territory has always been a subject of fascination for those of us in the East. Strange and wonderful tales were told of the region throughout the Nineteenth Century. Perhaps that is why our ancestors were so apt to accept Oregon as the birthplace of Ka-Ton-Ka, asserted by its makers to be one of the greatest boons ever offered to suffering humankind.

Ka-Ton-Ka was only one of thousands of patent medicines available to the American public around the turn of the century, but it was more popular than most. Although it was never pushed as a panacea for all diseases, it was certainly touted as a "perfect remedy" for a good many of them, including headaches, disorders of the liver and kidney, malaria, rheumatism, dyspepsia, "female complaints," gravel or stones in the bladder, barrenness, and pain in the back. The wonderful properties of Ka-Ton-Ka, said an advertising brochure, were entirely due to the fact that all ingredients were "gathered by the Warm Springs Indians in Oregon and Washington Territory. They prepare them in their own peculiar manner; and no druggist can duplicate that simple Indian preparation from his extensive stock of drugs, and all his experience and knowledge combined." Ka-Ton-Ka, its makers always pointed out, was an authentic Native American product. Its introduction was "the first time in the history of this country that a genuine Indian medicine was given to the public, gathered, prepared and sold by the Indians themselves."

In point of fact, Ka-Ton-Ka was less Indian than it was the product of the fertile imagination of "Colonel" T.A. Edwards, owner of the Oregon Indian Medicine Company out of Corry, PA. Edwards was one of those colorful characters who always seem to crop up when one does research in this period of American history. Born in New York State in 1832, Edwards got tired of farm life as a teenager and ran off to sea. A few years later he landed a job as business manager for the Spaulding and Rogers Circus. After doing similar work for the John Robinson Circus, he joined General Albert Sidney Johnston's campaign against the Mormons and, while in the West, participated in the Pike's Peak gold rush. Working his way back East, Edwards joined the nation's fledgling secret service just in time for the Civil War. His experience in that organization served him in good stead when, in 1866, he became a spy and messenger under General Cooke during the Snake Indian campaign.

It was at this time that Edwards established his Oregon connections by hooking up with Donald McKay, a trapper, scout, and self-proclaimed hero of the Modoc War. Raised in Oregon's Umatilla County, McKay was an authentic Western hero, as company publications never tired of pointing out. They described in great

detail his victory over the villainous Captain Jack and his party of renegade Indians. According to one pamphlet, "after two thousand soldiers and Oregon volunteers had been fighting the Modocs for seven months without making any impression, Donald McKay, with only seventy-one Warm Spring Indians, killed or captured the whole band." In addition to whatever prestige McKay could garner from his Modoc exploits, he possessed the advantages, so far as advertising copy went, of having an Indian mother and a brother, William, who was a physician and a graduate of Willamette College.

The Modoc War had received a big press in Eastern newspapers, and Edwards sensed an opportunity. Making use of his circus background, he teamed up with McKay and in 1874 toured Europe with Indians from the Warm Springs Reservation. Because of the Modoc campaign, Edwards billed his group as "The Heroes of the Lava Beds." Later the troupe arrived at Philadelphia in time for the Centennial of 1876. What caused Edwards to close the Indian show at this time is unclear. Perhaps the Modoc War had become too stale news. Perhaps he may have gotten the idea of switching from show business to the drug business because of his years with Dr. Gilbert Reynolds Spaulding, one of his first employers and an Albany druggist who had conceived of running a showboat down the Mississippi instead of tending his store. And perhaps Edwards was impressed with the success of other "Indian" medicines. At any rate, in the fall of 1876 Edwards and McKay started the Oregon Indian Medicine Company and commenced manufacturing a line of patent medicines, first in Pittsburgh, PA, then later in Corry.

Edwards was to claim that the miraculous efficacy of his products derived from the roots and mosses so laboriously picked by Warm Springs, Modoc, and Nez Perce women in Oregon. By the turn of the century as many as thirty-seven traveling groups, all supposedly staffed by Warm Springs Indians, were touring the Eastern states to hawk the company's products. In war paint and full "Stage Indian" regalia, they created quite a spectacle as they marched down the main streets of towns to their "encampments." They then attracted curious crowds to the "lecturers" by staging war dances and other entertainments. Actually, despite this hype, there is no evidence that the company ever used any materials from Oregon, or indeed anything besides custuming that was even specifically Native American.

The Indians in the shows, if they were indeed such, were more likely Mohawks and Senecas off reservations in the East. And some medicine show "Indians" are known to have been "Wannabees," swarthy types who "passed" for the sake of the money to be made. At least two immigrant Irishmen are reported to have done just that.

Not content with the profits from these itinerant troupes, Edwards also sold wholesale to druggists and, through ads in *The Billboard* and other publications, offered franchises to independent "managers and doctors." For a while business was very good. The heyday of the Oregon Indian Medicine Company was from 1880 to about 1918, when the Federal Pure Food and Drug Administration determined that Ka-Ton-Ka was really composed of "a mixture of alcohol, sugar, aloes, and baking soda." Before then Ka-Ton-Ka was the firm's largest selling medicine, though its 20% alcohol content probably had always contributed as much to its popularity as any supposed therapeutic benefits. For customers still uninterested in this "perfect remedy," there was of course a full line of other products. There was Modoc Oil, for instance, which was good for anything from cholera to deafness. Warm Spring Indian Moc-Ci-Tong was a specific for what the company euphemistically called "healthy secretions" or "manly and womanly capacity," and, "did not honor prevent, reference could be made to hundreds of the most prominent ladies and gentlemen in the Union who have been cured after all other treatment had failed." The company also produced War Paint Ointment, Indian Cough Syrup, Nez Perce Catarrh Remedy, and Donald McKay's Great Indian Worm Eradicator. In his entertaining book, *Step Right Up*, Brooks McNamara quotes a former company employee who participated in the manufacture of this last product. It seems that long strips of tissue paper were rolled into egg-shaped pills and dipped into a syrup which would become quite hard when dry. When the syrup dissolved in the body, the strip would then unwind in the digestive tract, eventually to become convincing proof to the patient that the "tapeworm" had met its end.

The Oregon Company had to produce such a long line of medicines in order to meet the competition, and there was plenty of that in the Indian medicine business. Indians in the Nineteenth century were considered by other Americans to be exceptionally healthy. They were, after all, very close to Nature. In addition, many of

their treatments were a part of the medical and historical literature. As early as 1534 the Huron Indian Dom Agaya had used a decoction of white pine or hemlock to cure Cartier's men of scurvy. Colonists, who themselves came from a rich herbal tradition, wrote down other indigenous medical uses for plants whenever they heard of them. John Wesley, later the founder of Methodism, was so impressed with Indian herb lore when he first came across it that he wrote a book about it called *Primitive Remedies*. In the preface to the book, which was first published in 1755 but went through many editions over the next century, Wesley wrote of the Indians that "their diseases indeed are exceedingly few; nor do they often occur, by reason of their continual exercise, and (till of late) universal temperance. But if any are sick, or bit by a serpent, or torn by a wild beast, the fathers immediately tell their children what remedy to apply. And it is rare that the patient suffers long; these medicines being quick, as well as generally infallible."

Public interest has waned in Indian medicine, and Americans are probably too sophisticated these days to fall for the more blatant pitches of the Indian show spielers. Nevertheless, there seems to be a renewed interest in the more authentic traditions of native herbalism. And, of course, there are some old-time products still available, like O-Jib-Wa Revitalizer from Flint, MI, or Rolling Thunder Kiowa Indian Mus-Ka-Bia from Steamburg, NY. But the shows that once pushed such products in every hamlet are long gone, and modern medicines of whatever sort have to pass far more governmental screening procedures than did their ancestors.

All in all, however, the hocum generated by the Nineteenth century medicine shows effectively destroyed the reputations Native Americans once had as great healers. Colonel Edwards was a major contributor to this loss of reputation. Yet he never seemed to suffer any consequences. He died in 1904, at the height of his company's success and fourteen years before Federal agents were to impound a shipment of Ka-Ton-Ka for false and fraudulent advertising. His funeral was a splendid affair, as befitted a city council member and leading businessman; according to the reporter for the local paper the obsequies were "the most largely participated in and impressive of any within our recollection." If the citizens of Corry, PA were ever embarrassed by Edwards' exaggerated claims for his products, they never showed it.

Early Days of Deschutes Junction

By Martha Stranahan

Once upon a time . . .

A townsite named Deschutes (Junction) from the early 1900s to the early 1930s embraced a hotel, railroad depot, irrigation district office, blacksmith shop, telephone office, store, two schools, post office, golf club, about 20 farm homes, residents poor and wealthy, flamboyant, steadfast, shakers, followers.

Homes, residents, businesses—all new, still cluster around Deschutes Junction, but they have little connection to the previous. A couple of houses, the tracks, a rude maypole in a former school yard, trees, a dirt road that might have been a freight route . . . and fragmented memories . . . remain.

A news item in the March 5, 1931 Bend Bulletin said "the last chapter in the history of Centrallo (latter day name for Deschutes, about midway between Bend and Redmond and east of the highway) is being written this month in a series of legal notices . . . . The only buildings . . . the Deschutes Hotel and the old Central Oregon Irrigation District office (and the land) . . . are being offered for sale for $100.00 . . . .

"Deschutes (then still in Crook County) was laid out in 1911 by the Deschutes Townsite Company . . . ." C.M. Redfield, engineer, filed July 11. Fred S. Stanley was president, Jesse Stearns secretary. (Several years

The Deschutes Hotel.

Photo courtesy of the Bend Bulletin and the Deschutes Historical Society.

earlier, pioneers had given that name to a very short-lived community just south of the present Bend.)

Oregon, Cascade, Deschutes, Jefferson and Cornell Avenues were platted to parallel the Oregon Trunk railway track; Juniper, Caledonia, Shasta, Klamath, Wenatchee, Columbia and Ash were right angle streets.

Irrigation and the railroad were the impetus for the community with a view of the Cascades.

Historians Keith and Donna Clark, Redmond, said old records indicate the Pilot Butte Development Company was formed October 31, 1900 by A.M. Drake to irrigate orchards, gardens and outlying areas of pioneers beginning to settle on and near the Deschutes River in the region of future Bend. Drake applied under the new Carey Act whose intent was to open western land to irrigation and cultivation.

In 1904 the Deschutes Irrigation and Power Company absorbed the PBD (also G.C. Hutchinson's Oregon Irrigation Company founded in 1898). Late in 1910, the DIPC conveyed titles and interests to the Central Oregon Irrigation Company, and in August 1921, the COIC transferred control of its canal system to the Central Oregon Irrigation District which had become a legal corporation in November, 1917.

Details of these transactions, of systems' construction, ownerships and management of water allocation and users, of legal ramifications and implications fill volumes in state and district offices.

Stanley was one of the "movers." Born in Chippewa Falls, Wisconsin in 1864, he (and his family) had

Store at Deschutes.

Photo courtesy of the Bend Bulletin and the Deschutes Historical Society.

extensive interests in timber, ranching, and banking in various central and eastern Oregon areas. In 1907 he traveled by auto caravan from Shaniko to Klamath Falls to meet railroad builder Edwin Henry Harriman. Four axemen cleared the road for the four-day trip. Stanley moved to Deschutes in 1917 and died there suddenly July 13, 1928.

The late J.L. Van Huffel, former Bend garage owner, was his chauffer and friend until his death.

Another Deschutes pioneer was Roscoe Howard who became Stanley's associate in irrigation development. He was the COIC general manager but in 1917 took leave to enter the Navy, whereupon Stanley, who was president, moved to Deschutes "to devote his entire time to management, which seemed necessary," according to old district records.

War years apparently were tough for selling water rights, and bonds for system improvement. Employees were asked to work "free" for a period. Among them were George Holton, Ole Hansen and W.P. Gift. However, they devised a water measuring rule that the district adopted. Settlers were "hostile," Stanley told his board in 1918. There was talk of trying to sell the system. In 1921 the COIC moved its headquarters to Redmond. (Employees lived in the Deschutes Hotel. In 1931 it was razed, along with the COIC office.) By 1924 district business was "picking up," and irrigation and cropping began to flourish.

In 1912 Howard built a magnificent three-story home north of the business area, that now is owned and lived in, and the land farmed, by Jack and Carol Nelson and their family. Old plans also show Howard as builder in 1912 of the Deschutes Hotel, with three floors, which Stanley later owned and operated.

Former Deschutes residents, many living in nearby cities, have special memories of that handsome hotel, as well as other events and customs in and around the town that never grew up to its streets. There were banquets, "fancy parties" and dances in the hotel's "beautiful ballroom," many given by Bend and Redmond hosts;

town ballgames on the school yards; three-act plays, musicals and socials in the school.

The W.K. McCormacks built the first school, "under the hill." It burned one night in 1924, and classes were held in the store until parents built a replacement on another location two years later. Early teachers included Ella Conway Smith, Nell Mahoney, Anna Moore Westerson and Genevieve Gedney. Families donated garden produce, children peeled vegetables and teachers cooked noon lunches on a potbelly stove. For some youngsters, it was the best meal of the day.

Willie and Hans Hansen; their sister, the late Elizabeth (Hansen) Miller; Harold Povey, Redmond; his brothers Victor, Portland, and Robert (deceased); Eva Susac (Lennox), Bend, were among the students. There were families of Mallery, Parks, McKnight, Simpkens, O'Donnell, Stadter, Mikkelsen and others.

Most settlers built their homes, some devised water systems. The hotel had its own, but there was a community reservoir about a mile to the south that fed water by gravity flow. Home generators made electricity. Meat was hung in trees to keep cool. There were some "tragic fires" Eva Lennox recalled—barns, sheds, houses. Once a man shot his family and set the house afire. The Ayer store (and post office) burned in 1914, with mail and fixtures saved but groceries and personal effects destroyed.

A sequence of abstracts on the Howard property shows it was deeded by the United States to the State of Oregon, January 8, 1908. In 1911 the state granted it to Howard. Subsequent owners were W.K. McCormack, 1919; E.O. Stadter, 1924; W.L. O'Donnell, 1932; Harry VanArsdale, 1940; Lloyd Crenshaw, 1965; Harvey L. Gillworth, 1969; Roderick B. Groshong, 1970; James G. Miller, 1972; Arlene Ibey, 1976; Arlene M. and Richard R. Ibey, 1979, and the Nelsons late in 1979. In 1940-43, New york entertainer and musician, Kay Swift, and her husband, Faye Hubbard, lived in the Howard house, ran livestock and held rodeos. (She was *not* of the Swift packing firm family.)

Lifestyles butted head-on. Women giggled about her going to "town," (Redmond) wearing a mink coat, jeans and boots or high heels (ho, hum). She published a book titled *"Who Could Ask For Anything More?"* The "anything" was her cowboy husband whom she had corralled when he "fell into" her box at Madison Square Garden.

Above Left: John Susac and daughter, Eva Lennox.
Above Right: 1912 home built by Roscoe Howard, now owned by Jack and Carol Nelson.

Martha Stranahan Photos (above).

Central Oregon Irrigation Co. Building.   Photo courtesy of the Bend Bulletin and the Deschutes Historical Society.

In thin fiction (DeLancey and Juniper Junction) for the river and community, she cuttingly parodied and caricatured their neighbors, rousing indignation and hurt feelings. "I didn't like her," several still recall. None deny, however, that she did bring lively music and music instruction to the schoolchildren. "Swifty" might not have realized the cruelty of her cleverness.

On the morning of July 13, 1928, Fred Stanley came to Ted and Min Povey's home. He wanted to talk to Povey, a plumber, who was away on a job. That night Stanley died at his home.

"I've always wondered what it was he wanted to see Ted about," Mrs. Povey said.

The railroad was a daily companion and public transportation for Deschutes. Frances McCormack Short Allen remembered riding between Redmond and Deschutes when she went to high school. And John Susac remembered "the day Fred Stanley's body went by on the train from Bend to Portland.

"He was a fine old gentleman. The people that he helped the most betrayed him. After he died, the hotel closed."

Susac was born in Austria, March 17, 1891. He came to the United States and "met a girl in Portland in 1910." He barbered "in practically every state in the union" and in 1919 opened his Metropolitan barber shop in Bend. He bought the Redfield home and land at Deschutes in 1929 and moved his wife, Elizabeth, and daughter, Eva (Lennox) there in 1930, when she was in fourth grade.

He commuted to his Bend barbershop and began to raise potatoes on the newly irrigated land. He "worked hard" and grew prize spuds, winning first in 1952 at Merrill. His wife died in 1958 and he stayed five more years at Deschutes. "I'd be there still if she were alive." He's 93, lives in Bend with his widowed daughter.

(The Redfield-Susac house not far from the Howard place is the other of the two remaining and occupied.)

"I remember the COI office building, the hotel, barn, depot, the tool shed and Fairbanks scale. People were living in the hotel and the COI building," Susac said in a 1982 interview. "I remember Roscoe Howard, Charlie Jones, Barney O'Donnell, E.O. Stadter, Tony Halter . . . ."

"You know, they tore down the buildings. We wondered why . . . only $500 taxes against them. Povey, Hansen and I had an idea we'd buy the whole property. I told them some day the highway will go through between Redmond and Bend, straight as the crow can fly. And the country's going to go wet! I said if those things materialize we could make $20,000 to $30,000 apiece. But they were torn down . . . ."

The March 5, 1931 Bend Bulletin continued, "about three years ago a determined effort to sell the hotel and 40 acres of land to Deschutes County as a poor farm was started," but dropped.

Taxes had lapsed in 1923 and again in 1924 and the county foreclosed. W.C. Moore, Redmond, was employed to strip the buildings of furnishings, plumbing fixtures, most of the doors and windows. He offered to buy the building shells and complete the wrecking, but did not want the land or tax liabilities. The court voted to offer the lots and buildings for sale for $100 minimum plus sale costs.

Moore—or someone—did raze the hotel and office. Some of the bricks were used in one or more Redmond buildings, and reputedly a house near the Bend drive-in theatre. In the 1950s Deschutes slipped toward ghost town but today there's new life and commerce around.

The railroad was a daily companion and public transportation for Deschutes. Frances M. S. Allen remembered riding between Redmond and Deschutes when she went to high school.

MOST UNIQUE CROSSING
Continued from Page 19

loosing stock to the Indian night raiders. Only once did the raiders touch his stock, and the next morning he met a group of Indians he had befriended driving the animals back to his wagon.

No man on the Oregon Trail was more highly respected by the Indians than Dr. Keil. They showered him with gifts and urged him to live with them. In his letters Keil wrote: "My greatest joy on the plains was meeting the Indians."

On November 1st, 1855, five months and one week after leaving Bethel, his wagon train arrived at Willapa Bay in Washington. They averaged 12½ miles a day including all stops. Not one life was lost. Every wagon that left Bethel arrived in Washington.

The body of Willie Keil was not buried until the day after Christmas. His grave marks the spot where the first pioneer was buried and the conclusion of the most fantastic wagon crossing ever made in America. But most of all it stands as a monument to fidelity; where a father fulfilled a promise to his son.

The Blue Mountain Fleet

By David H. Grover

One of the rewards of a trip through the old mining districts of the Blue Mountains is a chance to see the ramshackle ruins of the gold dredge at Sumpter. This experience is more than a view of a weathering hulk of wood and metal; it is a glimpse into the recent past, a colorful era when technology was writing the epilogue to the mining frontier.

Dredges played an important role in the life of several mining areas in the mountain valleys of Eastern Oregon during the first half of the twentieth century. Since much of the gold in the area occurred as placer gold which had washed out of the mountains, dredging was widely utilized on both sides of the Blue Mountains as the most efficient large-scale means of extracting the rare metal from the sand and gravel in which it had been deposited.

The greatest use of dredging came in the 1930's and 1940's when most gold mines had already been exhausted. Without these unique mechanical mosters digging their way across the landscape in search of wealth, gold mining would not have survived as long as it did in Oregon, and the economy of the area would have been adversely affected.

In Grant County on the western side of the Blue Mountains dredges worked on the valley floor at John Day, as well as on tributary streams such as Canyon Creek, and in the eastern part of the county at Granite. On the other side of the mountains in Baker County dredges operated near Sumpter and McEwen in the Powder River watershed, and on tributaries of the Burnt River in the southern part of the county.

Although gold dredges dug in the gravel deposited by streams, they generally did not actually float in the swift streams. Instead, they dug ponds around their hulls which were

filled by ground water or by water pumped in from the streams. In this way dredges created a serene and manageable floating environment that they could take along with them

LOWER LEFT: The remains of the dredge at Sumpter, well-worth a side trip into the mining district of the Blue Mountains, convey a sense of the size and power of these monsters of placer mining.
Oregon Historical Society Photo

LOWER RIGHT: This dredge worked at John Day before being dismantled and shipped off to a new assignment in Nevada.
Oregon Historical Society Photo

RIGHT: The business end of a gold dredge was its endless chain of buckets that brought the gravel onboard for washing and gold recovery.   California State Library Photo

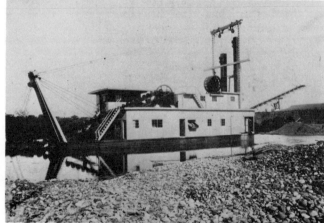

as they dug, by simply excavating material ahead of them and filling in behind. They could even work their way uphill or downhill merely by changing the level of the water in the pond.

Oregon dredging companies were fortunate in having adequate supplies of water for the dredge ponds. In some states the supply of water was a chronic problem, restricting the ability of the dredge to work in a pond that was deep enough to utilize fully the digging capability of the dredging equipment, which could go as deep as 100 feet.

Most gold dredges in the Pacific Northwest were of the bucket-ladder design in which a continuous chain of buckets dug into the underwater bank of the pond. Bucket capacities varied from 3 to 20 cubic feet, with 40 to 80 buckets on the chain moving at a speed of 10 to 20 buckets a minute.

Dredges were positioned in their ponds by means of winch-controlled mooring wires made fast to heavy weights on the shore called deadmen. The bucket ladders were held in contact against the sloping bank of the pond by the force exerted by long pilings known as spuds that were driven into the bottom of the pond through fittings on the stern of the hull.

Early dredges in remote locations sometimes used steam power or internal combustion engines to run the positioning winches and ladder-drive machinery, but electricity was the standard source of power by the time that dredging had become widespread.

Recovery of the gold took place aboard the dredge, using techniques similar to those in general use in other

In recovering gold aboard the dredge, the rotating trommel washed the finer material free for further treatment and sent the gravel on its way up the stacker to the bank of the pond.   California State Library Photo

types of placer mining. The gravel brought up in the buckets was dumped into a hopper from which it entered a rotating cylinder called a trommel. Inside the trommel, water

jets loosened the lighter material which went on to further processing while the heavier rock was sent on its way to the tailings dump at the edge of the pond by means of the conveyor belt on the stacker, the long boom protruding from the stern.

As the waste rock was being ejected behind the dredge, the slurry containing the gold in suspension was moving through a series of pulsating jigs, riffles, and mercury-covered amalgam tables for collection. The recovered gold, 80-90% pure with other metals as impurities, was then sent ashore for further refining.

In the heyday of dredging, with gold priced at $20-35 per ounce, dredges could make money working in deposits which contained only 10¢ worth of gold per cubic yard. Even today, 50¢ per cubic yard is considered the break-even point in dredging for gold worth $350 per ounce.

With this potential for profit, it is easy to see why dredging was attractive to mining companies. Whether dredging was attractive to the public, however, was a matter of local circumstances. Public acceptance of dredging was, at best, mixed. The people of Sumpter had a comfortable relationship with their dredge — it provided a steady payroll for the mountain community for many years without bringing in the tough social element often associated with mining camps. But, by contrast, in the John Day Valley some of the ranchers deeply resented the dredges to which some of the valley floor pastureland had been surrendered.

Although dredges moved at the proverbial snail's pace while earning money for their owners, they could be highly mobile at other times. Most dredges were erected at their dredging site, using modular construction that permitted them to be dismantled and moved to other locations by truck or rail when their work was completed.

The abandoned dredge at Sumpter was an exception to the vagabond nature of dredges. After 40 years of service its owners must have felt that their investment in the wooden-hull vessel was fully depreciated, so they retired it on the spot. Although an occasional dredge hulk can be found in Montana, Colorado, and Idaho — where one is now being preserved as a tourist attraction by a local historical association — dredges were generally not abandoned, but were simply moved to another location. This is particularly true of those with modular construction and steel hulls. The larger and more efficient dredges often ended their careers in South

America or in Southeast Asia.

Unfortunately, today there are no more domestic locations to which to move an out-of-work dredge. Gold dredging has virtually disappeared in the United States, surviving only in California where a single dredge is operating, and in Alaska where four are still at work. Ironically, virtually all dredges never had the opportunity of digging for high-priced gold which came along after the general demise of dredging.

In spite of their efficiency, it is unlikely that dredges will make a comeback in Oregon. There are just too many tailing piles still left, silently reminding the public of the environmental effects of bygone dredging, to make the resurrection of dredging as easy to achieve politically as it is to justify economically. Unlike California, Nevada, and, to a lesser degree, Montana, where dredging occurred in relatively uninteresting areas from a scenic point of view, much of the dredging in Oregon took place in some particularly beautiful areas that many people would now be unwilling to turn back to the dredging companies.

Even though dredges can be operated in such a way as to restore the land to its original condition, there is a price tag for such restoration, a total cost that often includes expensive litigation. The overall cost to the mining companies may be more than they are willing to assume.

Interest remains high in gold, however, and the widespread occurrence of placer deposits in the Blue Mountains, together with the fact that tailings piles are often reworked periodically by mining companies as gold recovery techniques improve, suggest that there may yet be a future for the gold dredge in Oregon. But, to use that classic good advice, don't hold your breath, waiting for the Blue Mountain fleet to reappear.

LEFT: The Bend railroad station was built in 1911, when the rails finally reached the Central Oregon town. Prosperity quickly came with it as wool, timber and cattle came from all over the region for shipment.   Norman Barrett II Photo

Little Known Tales from Oregon History

No. 38

Follow the Rails

By Norman M. Barrett

The pale sunlight forced its way through the heavy haze. The rising sun's weak warmth barely took the chill edge off the morning air. With old railroad maps lying alongside the new highway map, and books scattered around the car, we planned our excursion for the day.

A 1926 railroad map showed that Sprague River was the end of the line for the Oregon, California and Eastern Railroad. End of the line might mean a railroad station. That would be our first stop. After that we would work up the east side of the Cascades, as far as Bend.

My father's interest in the railroads dated back many years. With his retirement he suddenly had free time to explore them in depth. High on his agenda was a search for the old stations around the country. With the steady decline of railroad passenger service, many of the stations had long

since been torn down. Others were abandoned and would soon enjoy the same fate. The few that remained active were falling into disrepair. Now was the time to save them, at least on film, before they all vanished completely.

Weeks before the trip he visited the library. Here, armed with histories of railroads and eastern Oregon, he began looking at possible towns to visit. Any town, no matter how small, deserved a look if it had ever been on a rail line. Many of the original towns along the railroads didn't even exist any more.

Major railroads, like the Union Pacific, had lines through eastern Oregon while numerous small, private companies had also put in lines. The city of Prineville even built their own railroad. The easiest way to find the stations was to simply follow the rails.

Highway 140 wound up over Bly Mountain and down into the Sprague River Valley. The turnoff to Sprague

River led us through fertile ranch land with scattered herds of cattle dotting the landscape. Rough-legged hawks warily watched us pass from their high perches atop the telephone poles. The small town of Sprague River bordered a bend in the road, a small distance from the river itself.

We found that the best places for gathering information in a small town are the gas stations and the cafes. We chose the cafe. Over a generous slab of peach pie and a cup of coffee, we talked with the owners. There had never been a station in Sprague River, we found out. They had that on the best of authorities— some of their patrons had lived there since the town was formed. No, never was one.

We wondered, out loud, why the spur came to the town. This they did know. Sprague River was lumber country and the spur was put in to take the logs out. There was a loading area, now run by Weyerhauser, but there had never been passenger service.

Specialized spur lines, like this one, wander all over eastern Oregon, and were closely tied to its early development. The rivers were unsuitable for shipping. Wagon transportation was extremely expensive. Until a cheap way to ship goods was found, most of the resources of the Oregon interior could not be developed. Towns like Sprague River needed the railroads to move their timber, wool or cattle. Until the railroads came, no town could really develop.

Klamath Falls had train service early in its history, and it is one of the few places in eastern Oregon to still have passenger service. We returned to Klamath Falls to search out their depot. At least here we knew we wouldn't be disappointed. Amtrak stopped in Klamath Falls and there had to be a station. One of our books showed a photograph of a two-story building with stone pillars. It looked like a station we would want to see, if we could find it.

The Amtrak stop proved to be a small, rectangular building that was the common design in the early part of the 1900's. We walked around and photographed it from several sides. It is one of the lucky stations. Service still stopped there and the station would remain.

The larger station wasn't in sight, so we drove down the tracks. The Klamath County Historical Museum was a few blocks away and we stopped to talk. These museums are a well of information waiting to be tapped. We took in our book and showed the picture to the ladies at the front counter. They immediately recognized the station.

"Oh, I'm sorry," one of them told us. "Union Pacific tore that building down two years ago." As had been the fate of so many stations, it had stood empty for too long. Nobody wanted it and it was an unneeded expense.

We had arrived too late to preserve that depot on film. The disappointment only served to spur us on in search of others before they were destroyed. We followed the rails.

From Klamath Falls the tracks led north to Chemult, where they turned west to cross the Cascades. A stop at Chiloquin turned up nothing. Beaver Marsh was the same. Chemult was listed as an Amtrak stop. Perhaps our luck would improve.

We spotted Amtrak's sign as we pulled into Chemult and followed the arrow to the right. In the parking lot we were greeted by the raucous call of a Clark's nutcracker, perched in a fir tree. He is a fitting welcomer to any visitors leaving the train here, because Chemult is Amtrak's gateway to Crater Lake and the high Cascades.

The depot is as basic as you will ever find, an open platform beside a parking lot. There is no shelter and no other comforts, but the train does stop. Across the tracks, separate from the passenger platform, stands an old station. With cracked paint and weathered wood, it appears abandoned, but the radio tower and beaten path to the door argue otherwise.

We swung away from the tracks as they turned west. Our final destination for this trip would be Bend. Stops at Crescent and Gilchrist showed nothing. If railroads ever came to these towns, they were long gone and forgotten.

We rejoined railroad tracks at LaPine as they swung up toward Bend from the south-

TOP: The Chemult station stands across the tracks from the Amtrak platform. It is the basic rectangular architecture found in most rural stations. The bay window on the track side allows the station master to watch for the trains in both directions. Norman Barrett II Photo

CENTER: The Klamath Falls depot stays active with two daily stops by Amtrak. It is also the major shipping center for Southern Oregon and Northern California. Norman Barrett II Photo

LOWER RIGHT: Before Bend had rail service, Shaniko's small station served as the major shipping point in Central Oregon. George W. Linn Photo

east. A station? The gas station attendant seemed to recall one but he was sure it had been torn down long ago. Where? He pointed east, down a country road that ran straight into nowhere. "Follow that until you hit the tracks."

Follow it we did, out of town and into the country. When we reached the tracks we found a lonely railroad sign. Its faded paint proclaimed that this was LaPine. The silent forest denied it. The town wasn't even visible. There was nothing else, no station, no platform.

The rails led north and we followed. They pulled into Bend and we zig-zagged through side streets, trying to stay near them. Soon a station came

into view. With two stone pillars on the south end, it was the most elaborate station we had seen that day. A cornerstone proclaimed its age, 1911. Like the others, it showed the signs of age, but it showed something else. You could tell that it was used. It looked alive.

If this station was built in 1911, had there ever been an earlier one? I consulted a small map of the city and located the Historical Society. We drove to Reed School, now an historical museum, and sought the answer.

A couple of books in their library informed us that Bend was founded around 1904 and the railroad didn't arrive until 1910. The station we had found was the first.

Any book on the railroad history of eastern Oregon will lead you right into Prineville. Prior to 1900 Prineville was the major city in central Oregon. Built around cattle and sheep, it had only one problem. There was no easy way to ship goods in and out of the town. The rivers were unnavigable, the roads were long and rough, and the nearest railroad was along the Columbia.

The city longed for a railroad. They dreamed of the vast prosperity it would bring to the community. The railroads also dreamed of a line through central Oregon to connect the Northwest with California. Nothing came of many of the plans.

An East-West line, the dream of T. Egenton Hogg, was to run from Yaquina Bay, through Corvallis, over Santiam Pass to Prineville. From there it would continue east to Idaho. That dream died short of the summit.

Prineville's second dream was the Columbia Southern Railway. Starting at Biggs, on the Columbia, it was to head south to Prineville. 75 miles of track were laid and the railroad built a town at the end. This town, named Shaniko, quickly bloomed. Stage and freight lines radiated out in several directions, drawing in wool and beef from all over central Oregon. As for the tracks, they never went any further. A steep grade between Shaniko and Antelope was too difficult and costly to lay.

From the south came another railroad. The Nevada-California-Oregon Railway was going to connect Reno to the Columbia, while going through Prineville. This dream died with the end of the tracks in Lakeview.

During the 1890's the Great Northern and Union Pacific Railroads were looking for their own route through central Oregon. Both had their eyes on the Deschutes River Valley. An early survey in the 1850's had declared the gorge impossible as a railroad route. Technology had changed in the intervening 40 years

Any book on the railroad history of eastern Oregon will lead you right into Prineville. Prior to 1900 Prineville was the major city in central Oregon. Built around cattle and sheep, it had only one problem. There was no easy way to ship goods in and out of the town.

and it was now possible, but it would be expensive.

The two major railroads squared off to do battle. Prineville didn't care who won because the city couldn't lose. They would finally get their railroad.

The Great Northern (now the Burlington Northern) started laying track up one side of the gorge. The Union Pacific paced them up the other side. It was a literal war with dynamiting, sabotage, and pitched battles between the two companies. In 1910, with both sides financially drained, peace was reached. A compromise resulted in shared tracks and expenses. The tracks were laid and Prineville discovered it had lost. The tracks avoided their town and went through Farewell Bend, Oregon.

In later years the Farewell was dropped and Bend grew with the prosperity that the citizens of Prineville had expected. Prineville refused to be left out and die. If the railroads wouldn't come to Prineville, Prineville would build their own.

In August of 1918 the first train left Prineville on the city tracks. The trains have never stopped running and Prineville has the only railroad in the country that has been in continual city ownership. Prineville never had the prosperity they anticipated, but they did manage to survive. Other towns vanished when the tracks passed them by.

A simple search for the railroad stations had given us a new look at the history and development of our state. The tracks had created and destroyed towns. It had determined where the future would be. When it reached Bend, Bend prospered. With the mainline running north and south, business went to Bend. Shaniko, on its small spur, died. Prineville survived only by building their own spur to the mainline.

We returned the books to the shelves and left the museum. Our day was ending and we were due home. Prineville and Shaniko would have to be another trip.

My father had more research ahead. What tracks had been laid and then removed? Did any of the stations along those lines still exist? An earlier trip across the country had found railroad stations that had been converted into houses, restaurants, motels, and even junk shops. Even with the tracks gone, the stations might still exist. Only bookwork and time would uncover them.

We followed the rails back to the south. A southbound freight ran beside us for a way and then swung east. What stations would it see?

Fireside Stories from Native Americans

Text and Cartoons by John Simpson

Imagine Central Oregon as a place where mountains move and where spirits dwell in lakes. It is a place of mystery and power; where the stories are both teachers and entertainers. Often they are stories of this place before man came to dwell, and they talk of the formation of mountains, lakes, rivers. They tell stories of the love, hate and war among giant people of times long, long past.

These tales are very ancient. It is easy to forget that until just 100 years ago the land belonged to Native American people; people who enjoyed a lifestyle unchanged for a long, long time and with that lifestyle, their stories.

Imagine yourself sitting by the flickering embers of a fire. It is warm inside and the evening is long. A face is illuminated by the flames. He says that the mountains were once people. Giant people that moved. Giant people with love and jealousy.

Once Mount Adams, north of the big river, the Columbia, and Mount Hood on the other side, became jealous of each other. It was the jealousy over a girl. At that time, there was a bridge over the river. This made it possible for the two giants to cross over to fight.

Mt. Hood socks Mt. Adams in the nose after crossing the Columbia River.

Coyote, who sometimes tried to make things right in the world, tried but could not get them to stop the battles. So, he talked to the other mountain people to help. They agreed. From deep down in Klamath country to the south, the mountain giants marched north. They would cross the Columbia on the bridge for a meeting on the north side. The Three Sisters and Black Butte were among them.

Coyote was impatient as usual. He could not wait for the mountain people to come to the Columbia. He thought he would solve the crises himself and set about to break the bridge across the Columbia before the next big

wrestling match between the mountains. Coyote found the bridge and broke it, and when the mountain people heard of this, they stopped their march northward.

Coyote breaks down the bridge over the Columbia River.

When they heard this news, Black Butte and her husband were resting. It was very hot and Black Butte was carrying a big bag of roots and berries for food along the way. When they heard the news of Coyote breaking the bridge, they decided to stay. Black Butte was very tired and so warm that sweat ran down her face and sides. It ran down in streams and rivers. She is still cooling off from that long march, because the streams of sweat collect below her and form the Metolius River. It takes a long time to cool down if you are a mountain that can move. And Black Butte brought plenty of food then, because she still carried many, many edible roots and berries which can be found on her back today.

And Klah Klahnee came on the march too. Klah Klahnee means "Three Points". Klah Klahnee was once not three points but one giant mountain. It was bigger than any others in the range. Maybe it too was hot from the march northward, because one day the earth shook for days. The mountain boiled inside until hot rocks poured from its side. Fire and smoke blasted from its top, burning many people and destroying villages. Finally, the mountain grew quiet, but most of it had disappeared. The mountain must have been a huge mountain, because all that was left were three points. Klah Klahnee, "Three Points", is better known as the Three Sisters today.

Another story teller enters the stage formed by the fire's flickering light. He tells a story about a flood, yet this was not just one flood, but three. Once it rained forever until water covered the land. These waters finally flowed away. Then another flood came and took the land again. It too left after a long, long time.

To get ready for yet another flood, the people cut the biggest cedar they could find. From this giant log, they built the biggest canoe anyone had ever seen. And yes, another flood came, but this time the people chose the bravest and best of the young for the canoe. They put these young people in the canoe with enough food to last the flood. But this flood took nearly all of the land, it was very deep.

When the clouds finally left them, they could see only a small point of land. They paddled to it and landed. The flood waters receded, and they found themselves resting on the top of a giant peak. When the lowlands dried, they left the canoe and made for their old lands. The canoe still sits atop the mountain now called Mount Jefferson. You can see it sticking out of the very top of an otherwise flat-topped peak.

Stories adapted from Indian Legends of the Pacific Northwest.
Ella E. Clark, University of California Press

Remembering Homer Davenport

By David Braly

His work still appears. No longer in The Oregonian or the other newspapers which used to run it. It's in the history books now, an attempt by editors to reveal the political passions and disputes of a bygone age. Homer Davenport died 73 years ago, and the age he observed and recorded did not long survive him. But that's another story. The important thing is that Homer Davenport died in New York City and that was a long way from Silverton, Oregon.

He was born near Silverton in 1867 and raised there on the family farm. His mother died when he was 3. His father and grandfather were both physicians. And his father was more: he was a county surveyor, state land agent, a writer of articles for medical journals, and a member of the Oregon Senate. Homer learned about politics early.

Homer's early life wasn't much different from any other boy growing up in Oregon during the last half of the 19th Century. He did farm chores until his father moved into Silverton when Homer was 7, and then he worked in a store, did odd jobs, and raised chickens. In his spare time he drew pictures and played cornet.

In view of his subsequent career, it is perhaps odd that Homer Davenport's first ambition was to be a businessman. But that was his goal and he made several attempts to pursue it. He even attended a business college in Portland for a brief time. He dropped out, enrolled in an art school, but quit that too.

A friend of the Davenport family who knew about Homer's artistic ability, Hollister McGuire, urged the young man to make his living as a cartoonist. This was at a time when Thomas Nast and other political cartoonists were reaching the peak of their influence and power. Homer decided to give it a try and secured a job on the Portland Mercury as staff artist and cartoonist. In 1889 he managed to get a job with The

Homer Davenport

Oregonian, but it didn't last and soon he was back in Silverton. He became a brakeman for the Northern Pacific Railroad.

Homer Davenport's love of animals is what took him out of Silverton and into the turbulent world of national affairs. He took a job tending animals belonging to a small circus, and his work took him to San Francisco. A display of his cartooning ability won him a job on William Randolph Hearst's San Francisco Examiner.

Hearst found in Davenport an artist who could render a political cartoon as brilliantly as his prize writer Ambrose Bierce could render a column. He frequently teamed them, especially to assault C.P. Huntington. As head of the Southern Pacific, Huntington in those days was virtual dictator of California's entire transportation network. He was also perhaps the most hated man in the state, therefore the one Hearst could sell the most newspapers by attacking. During the three years that Davenport worked for the Examiner he satirized Huntington so often that his caricatures of the

tycoon became more familiar than the actual photographs of him.

While living in San Francisco, Davenport met Daisy Moore. He married her in Chicago. They had two children, but their marriage was an unhappy one and they later separated.

Hearst transferred Davenport to the New York Evening Journal in 1895, and it was his cartoons for that newspaper that made Davenport famous nationally. They attacked the gold standard, Republican presidential candidate William McKinley, Mark Hanna, and the trusts. His depiction of Hanna as a fat mogul wearing a suit covered with dollar signs and of McKinley as the servant of Hanna and the trusts created a furor among Republicans and top executives of the country's largest corporations.

McKinley won the election, but the damage done his cause by Davenport was not forgotten. At the next session of the New York Assembly a bill was introduced to prohibit newspapers from publishing cartoons. Proponents argued that the cartoons portrayed individuals libelously, doing things that they never did (Mark Hanna, embraced by an ugly caveman who represented the trusts, wearing a $-covered suit); opponents said that cartoons were a form of political and journalistic expression and as such protected by the U.S. Constitution. After a long, bitter battle, the anti-cartoon bill failed.

Some Davenport cartoons are still famous. Notable among these are "The Boss," depicting Sam Rainey; "Lest We Forget," showing Admiral Dewey's victory at Manila Bay, published at a time when Dewey was under public censure for having given to his wife a house presented to him by admirers; a cartoon showing Uncle Sam (who Davenport could render better than any other cartoonist) holding the hand of the wounded McKinley; and "He's Good Enough for Me!," a cartoon drawn for

Uncle Sam

Mark Hanna, and the trust "brute"

the New York Evening Mail after Davenport had quite Hearst, showing Uncle Sam patting Theodore Roosevelt on the back at the time of the 1904 presidential election. Millions of copies of the latter cartoon were printed and distributed, and it can still be seen in some encyclopedias.

By now Homer Davenport had become one of the highest-paid cartoonists in history. He made money not only from his cartoons, but also from humorous lectures about his Silverton boyhood, his travels, and the role of the cartoonist, and from six books which he wrote and published: "Cartoons" (1989); "The Bell of Silverton" (1899); "Other Stories of Oregon" (1900); "The Dollar or the Man?" (1900); "My Quest of the Arab Horse" (1909); and "The Country Boy" (1910). He bought a farm near Morristown, N.J., where, true to form, he kept all sorts of animals, only some of which belonged on a farm. He traveled to Europe (where he made caricature studies at the Dreyfus trial) and the Middle East (where he drew Arab men and Arab horses). He also traveled to Oregon, where reporters from The Oregonian intereviewed their former colleague.

Although he rejoined the Hearst organization as cartoonist for the New York American, Davenport retained the gratitude of President Roosevelt for his "He's Good Enough for Me!" cartoon. When T.R. learned about Davenport's yearning and long quest for an Arabian horse, he personally wrote to the Sultan of Turkey and obtained for him 27 of them. Davenport put the horses on his Morristown farm.

Davenport hadn't forgotten his roots. Many of his lectures were about Oregon and the good times he'd had there. He especially loved to talk about growing up in Silverton. He maintained many friendships with people in the state. He often sent original copies of his cartoons to Oregon friends as momentoes. In fact, a book of these original cartoons was compiled from 1945 to 1949 from drawings in the possession of Hollister McGuire's son and other individuals. Only five copies were produced, and none of them were for sale.

Homer Davenport died May 2, 1912. In life, however far he had wandered or risen, he had always returned to Oregon. To Silverton. It was the same in death: although Homer Davenport had died in New York, his body was returned to Silverton for burial.

Judge John B. Waldo:
Defender of the High Cascades

by Steve Knight

Judge John Breckenridge Waldo
(1844-1907)
Oregon Historical Society Photo

NORTH SHORE OF WALDO LAKE, OCT 4, 1985: A pre-industrial serenity reigns here, and it is easy to understand why Judge John B. Waldo would journey for days on horseback to camp at this High Cascades lake. The only sound I hear is a faint, wispy wind tossling the tops of nearby mountain hemlock. Waldo itself is bathed in the brilliant glow of a midday sun, and I am struck by the sharp contrast between the indigo lake and the surrounding forestland — a rich, green wilderness of old growth fir, pine and hemlock. Another stunning sight is Diamond Peak — dusted white from an early snowstorm — rising up over Waldo's south shore.

Nearly 100 years ago Judge Waldo stood on this very shore and described a similar pleasing scene:

"The lake looks beautiful embossed in the evergreen forests - dark timbered peninsulas jutting into it, with the broad snow fields of Diamond Peak and blue mountains looking down upon it," he wrote in his diary on Aug. 1, 1888.

The judge visited his eponymous namesake on many occasions and once took the liberty of stocking it with 100 small trout he had taken from nearby Crescent Lake.

Actually the 10 square mile lake was once called Pengra Lake, named for B.J. Pengra, a railroad and road building booster. By the 1880s, however, the name had changed to Waldo, possibly because many people began to associate Judge Waldo with the lake. One story has it that Pengra was incensed when hearing about the name change, but Waldo is probably the better name if for no other reason than to honor a man who truly loved the High Cascades of Oregon.

To Waldo, these wild mountains were a sanctuary from too much civilization, a place that enriched the human spirit and brought out the best qualities in man. In a letter from Odell on Sept. 4, 1980, he wrote:

Cannot the inspiration of the forest be traced in the development of Washington and Lincoln? The conditions which took them into the wilderness and brought them close to nature no doubt were directly responsible for much of the best in their characters.

John B. Waldo was a native Oregonian born in 1844. He studied law, graduated from Willamette University and was admitted to the Oregon State Bar in 1870. Ten years later he was elected to the Oregon Supreme Court. He also served briefly in the Legislature in 1889. Throughout these years in government and up until his death in 1907, Waldo was a steadfast defender of Oregon's "free and untrammeled wilderness."

In the late 19th century, Oregon's public lands were up for grabs. Waldo feared the High Cascades would be sold off to the highest bidder, in effect, taken out of the public domain and placed into the hands of unscrupulous land speculators. In 1889, he introduced legislation that asked Congress "to set aside and forever reserve. . . all that portion of the Cascade Range throughout the State, extending twelve miles on each side . . . of the summit of the range."

This one measure helped put much of the High Cascades into the National Forest System we know today.

Waldo could easily be called "the John Muir of Oregon." And it was the High Cascades of Oregon that he cherished. He had no desire to explore Yosemite Valley. Or the Grand Canyon. Or the Yukon. Paradise to Waldo was camping along some pristine Cascade lake.

And camping to Waldo wasn't just a leisurely jaunt into the wilds of Oregon. He and friends spent whole summers exploring the vast wildnerness tracts that stretched from Crater Lake to Mount Hood. Waldo usually left his Salem home in July and camped in the Cascades until late September.

His mode of travel was, of course, by horse, and because the trips lasted for months he also took a horse drawn supply wagon and pack animals. After leaving Salem, he and three or four companions would snake their way up a path along the Santiam River to Breitenbush hotsprings or swing through Eugene, hook onto the Central Military Wagon Road and head toward the Three Sister-Diamond Peak area.

Waldo Lake . . . one of the purest lakes in the world. This picture of solitude is essentially unchanged since Judge Waldo's visits over 100 years ago.

Photo by Diane Kelsay

These treks were more often than not fraught with hardships we modern outdoorsmen might find unbearable. In a July 20th, 1887 letter Waldo wrote:

More than a week was spent winding laboriously among labyrinths of fallen timber and climbing along the sides of mountains on trails frequently blocked by logs and which must be gotten over or around with danger and difficulty.

Not surprisingly accidents would inevitably occur. On one excursion, a packhorse was killed after tumbling down the side of a mountain. On another trip, Waldo strained his back so bad he couldn't ride his horse for two days. The judge also had periodic bouts with pleurisy which left him weak and unable to leave his sleeping bag. And then there were the calamities nature threw at Waldo's party: hailstorms, forest fires and clouds of mosquitoes.

Yet Waldo took all these mishaps in stride. He never complained. He could obviously bear any burden in a land "where every breath that blows inspires poetry." Then too he had the stamina and fortitude of some grizzled, old mountain man. He routinely cleared trails with a crosscut saw, killed deer, elk, black bear and "jerked" the meat, and went on 30 mile hikes before dinner.

At times Waldo appears overwhelmed by the profusion of wildlife in the High Cascades. Around every bend, it seems, he is spying osprey, loons, "white headed" eagles, deer, elk and black bear. Once he even spotted a grizzly bear near Mount Jefferson:

Away on the north side of Jefferson, remote from human intrusion, I saw a grizzly bear — genuine — such a huge monster of a bear could be nothing else but a grizzly. He. . . was about 200 yards distance, feeding, unconscious of any presence. I took one look at him through the (spy) glass and at once looked

around for safe retreat.

Wolves too roamed the High Cascades 100 years ago, and Waldo mentions seeing several in 1887 near the headwaters of the Middle Fork of the Willamette. The only creature Waldo rarely chances upon are humans. If there were people about, he certainly did not go out of his way to find them. The judge always made an effort to find campsites where he would not be "bothered by tramps or disturbed by visitors."

Waldo sought a wilderness experience in its wildest and purest form, and even in the late 19th century, it was still possible to find unexplored territory — away from people and civilization — in the Cascades. In fact Waldo's diary is filled with accounts of explorations and discoveries that read, in places, like excerpts from Lewis and Clark's journal: On August 24, 1880, Waldo and two friends got lost south of the Three Sisters and were forced to follow an Indian Trail.

Continued on Page 44

No. 42

Too Many Courthouses

By David Braly

Photos Courtesy of the Klamath County
Museum

It seemed simple to the Klamath County Court in 1909: they needed a new courthouse, so they would get one.

What they got were three courthouses and thirteen years of bitter controversy.

Klamath Falls was a boom town in 1909. The U.S. Department of Interior's Klamath Reclamation Project was converting the grazing land near the town into an agicultural empire. The arrival of the Southern Railroad had prompted the construction of sawmills.

The old courthouse on Main Street, built for $3500 in 1888, was inadequate for county needs. The county court decided to build a new two-story brick courthouse. It would have a jail in the attic and a foundation sufficient to hold another two stories should they be needed later.

This plan might have been implemented with everybody satisfied if not for the Klamath Development Company.

The Klamath Development Company was promoting a new subdivision called the Hot Springs Addition. And what would promote a subdivision better than having the county courthouse there? In January 1910 the Klamath Development Company offered the county a free five-acre parcel inside the Hot Springs Addition for building a new courthouse upon.

This offer angered downtown businessmen who wanted the courthouse close to their stores. They protested to the county court that the courthouse must be built inside Klamath Falls, the county seat, and that Hot Springs was outside the city limits. After voters chose the Hot Springs site in a special election the downtown group obtained an injunction barring construction of the courthouse there on the grounds that Hot Springs was

outside the county seat. In 1912, however, the Oregon Supreme Court overturned the injunction. It ruled that Klamath Falls was a community, not a platted piece of ground with definite boundaries.

By that time a new organization called the Commercial Club had offered the county a new courthouse site on Main Street. When the county court rejected it and awarded a contract to build the new courthouse in Hot Springs, the downtowners launched a recall drive against county judge William Worden. Worden easily survived it. The new courthouse rose in Hot Springs.

Lumberman R. N. Day then began filing lawsuits against the county for contracting illegal indebtedness. The Oregon Constitution said that no county could be more than $5,000 in

debt, but Klamath was already $280,000 in the red. Believing Worden, extravagant in spending money he didn't have, Day challenged the legality of almost all the warrants issued by the county since Worden took office. Other people sued the county. And still more people sued. By February 1914 — when county indebtedness was above a half million dollars — there were so many lawsuits filed that the county wasn't able to issue more warrants.

Meanwhile, a new amendment to the state constitution gave county judges six year instead of four year terms. Worden felt that he didn't have to seek reelection for two more years because of it. Other people felt that because Worden took office before the amendment was passed it did not apply to his current term. Marion

Hanks was of the latter opinion and ran for Worden's undefended seat. Hanks was elected. Worden said he was still judge.

Klamath County therefore had two courthouses and two county judges at one time. Finally the Oregon Supreme Court ruled that Hanks was the true judge.

When Hanks took office the Hot Springs courthouse was well advanced. The massive gray Greek-style building had cost $112,000 so far and needed less than half that amount of money to be finished. By now the public was happy that the controversy was over and most people were willing to accept the Hot Springs courthouse.

Then Hanks threw everyone a curve. Early in 1918 he awarded a builder J. M. Dougan of Portland a $131,775 contract to build a new courthouse next to the old Main Street courthouse that was still being used. Hanks said that architects who had examined the Hot Springs courthouse warned that it was structurally unsound.

Rage swept the community. A recall drive was launched against Hanks, and a lawsuit was filed to stop work on any courthouse other than the one in Hot Springs. Dougan — paid an advance of $41,548 — began building the third courthouse anyway.

Hanks was recalled in April and Robert Bunnell installed as the new county judge. Bunnell was committed to the Hot Springs courthouse. The county commissioners and he ruled that because there had been no funds in the county treasury budgeted for courthouse construction the contract with Dougan was nonexistant. Dougan was ordered to stop construction and the county court sued him for recovery of the $41,548 advance they said had been paid to him illegally.

Dougan ignored the county's order to cease work. He continued to build the third courthouse. Opponents of the Hot Springs site loaned him money to keep going.

Bunnell's court announced in July that it would sell the land upon which Dougan was building. An injunction issued by Circuit Judge F. N. Calkins of Medford stopped this plan. Calkins

UPPER LEFT: The original courthouse built in 1888.

LOWER LEFT: The controversial Dougan courthouse was used as an emergency hospital and a schoolhouse before being ruled as the official Klamath County courthouse.

ABOVE: The Hot Springs courthouse was deemed unsafe and destroyed. Political fighting doomed the building almost from the start.

also ordered that Dougan's work not be interfered with and that no work be done on the Hot Springs courthouse.

Dougan finished the new Main Street courthouse in February 1919. The county court said that the building belonged to Dougan, not to the county, because no contract existed between the county and him. He had built it upon county land without authority. The court refused to pay either Dougan or the architect who had designed the building. Dougan sued for payment.

Dougan's courthouse might have stood as unused as the Hot Springs courthouse. County officials and employees were anxious to move there from their cramped rooms in the old courthouse; the county court forbade anyone from moving next door. But the courthouse was used as an emergency hospital during the influenza epidemic of 1920 and then to hold the overflow from a Klamath Falls school.

The Oregon Supreme Court ruled late in 1920 that the Dougan courthouse was the official Klamath County courthouse. It ordered the county court to pay Dougan the balance owed him of $92,674.

The county court stubbornly approved new architectual plans for the Hot Springs courthouse and budgeted $50,000 for work on it. Judge Calkins filed an injunction forbidding resumption of work there. The county court decided to pay off Dougan, sell the new Main Street courthouse, and use the proceeds to finish construction of the Hot Springs courthouse. Calkins filed another injunction forbidding new work at Hot Springs.

In 1921 the Klamath Falls grand jury recommended that the Dougan courthouse's jail facilities be used to relieve the overcrowded jail in the city hall basement. Bunnell responded by budgeting $15,000 to ready the jail facilities in the Hot Springs courthouse.

Finally, the Klamath Development Company demanded its title deed returned. It said that the five acres upon which the Hot Springs courthouse stood had been given to the county on condition that a courthouse be built there. A building had been built, true, but it was unoccupied by the county government and therefore not a courthouse.

The county court sued the company to prevent it recovering title.

Judge G. F. Skipworth of Eugene, holding court in Klamath Falls in November, ruled against the county court. He declared that the Klamath Development Company should recover its deed because the true courthouse of Klamath County was the one built by Dougan.

Even then Bunnell did not give up the ship — uh, the courthouse. The county court appealed to the Oregon Supreme Court. The Supreme Court upheld Skipworth in September 1923.

That finally settled the bitter controversy.

Today the Dougan building is still Klamath County's courthouse. The old Main Street courthouse was converted into an apartment building.

And what about that "structurally unsound" Greek-style building known as the Hot Springs courthouse? Destroyed. And it only took 1,000 pounds of dynamite and 30 days to do it!

Captain Jack's Stronghold

By Joe Kraus

EDITOR'S NOTE—Although this story takes place in northern California, its principal participants came from Lake County in South Central Oregon and should be of interest to our readers.

You won't see it on most highway maps and travel books have long neglected it. But tucked away in the far northern corner of California is an historical spot which for well over two years took the attention of the entire nation. The names of the people who took part in the events became household words. And the debate on who was right and who was wrong continues today.

Situated within the Lava Beds National Monument near Tule Lake the place is noted as one of the most perfect natural fortifications to be found in the whole American continent. This fortification was to become known as Captain Jack's Stronghold.

It was here that the great Modoc Indian Chief Captain Jack led his people. And it was here, when you consider the number of enemies, that the United States fought one of its most costly wars. For months on end 50 straggly and tired Indian braves equipped with a few ancient muzzle loaders held off over a thousand fully equipped men of the U.S. Army.

Here, eons of years ago, nature first began to shape the area which was not only to become a sanctuary of safety for Indians, but a geological freak as well. Some time during those ages a volcano erupted scattering hot molten lava throughout the area.

Today disquised with tall grass and sage, the remains of that eruption exists as it did a hundred years ago in the days of Captain Jack. Here are rocky ridges that reach a height of 10 feet. Numerous caves, miniature valleys and canyons honeycomb the surface. Lava crests are open at the top which provide natural footpaths between them. Other natural depressions, ridges and lava bubbles provide well concealed sentry and lookout posts.

The setting of the confrontation between whites and Indians was laid in those days when the west was supposedly "tamed." Many of the Indians from throughout the nation were already on reservations. What battles there were, were scattered and although dramatic, not all that common.

Even in this northwest country, however, the problems didn't really begin until a treaty was signed with the Klamaths, the Modocs and the Ya-hoos-kin band of Snakes. The treaty, in which the Indians readily agreed, stipulated that the Indians surrender all their lands and accept a reservation in Lake County, Oregon.

What the Modoc Indians didn't know, however, was that all Indians would be placed together. After attempting to make good their intentions, it was soon obvious that the various tribes did not mix well. The Modocs had constant problems with their ancient enemies, the Klamaths.

White solutions to the problem was not acceptable. So the Modocs, pushed to their limit and reduced to near starvation, left the reservation. The band, under the leadership of the Modoc Chief Captain Jack returned to its old home on Lost River. Then for a time individual and small groups of Indians roamed the country at will, never causing the whites any particular problems. The Indians even came to the aid of the

community of Yreka, California on July 4, 1871, when the town was engulfed in fire. The Indians did good service at the engine and elsewhere, in aiding to fight the flames.

Seeing these Indians on the loose over the country, however, had alarmed many whites. And many charged the Modocs with crimes they did not commit. The few raids that were conducted were later proven to be by the Klamaths.

Although many Army men, including General E.R.S. Canby who knew the truth about the Modocs, spoke out in their behalf, it was to no avail. Reservation Superintendent F.B. Odeneal, in charge at the time, believed what he wanted and enlarging upon it said that the Modocs were nothing but desperadoes and foes to civilization. It was his report that the Indian Bureau accepted. Odeneal was given the authority to arrest the Modoc leaders and round up their followers, forcibly bringing them back to the reservation.

Even Odeneal, however, would not have ordered what was to follow—a surprise attack by an Army captain on the Indian camp. This left eight or nine warriors dead. It was the one incident that drove the rest into the sanctuary of the nearby lava beds. And it was the first of many incidents that started the Modoc Indian War.

The battle to take the lava beds began under the command of Lieutenent Colonel Frank Wheaton on January 17, 1873. It was cold and foggy that particular morning and the troops felt confident of victory. But as they advanced, three companies strong, their confidence had turned into fear of defeat. For no sooner had they set foot on Indian land when they were met with a sudden deadly fire. The first charge which started out in a run and then to a brisk walk was soon no better than a crawl.

The fighting raged throughout the

OPPOSITE: Wildflowers bloom today where a century ago men died. Hill in background was known as Hospital Rock where the wounded Army men were taken after a battle.

ABOVE: National Park Service trails (like this one) follow the paths of Indians in their pursuit of Army patrols.

BELOW: Gillem's Camp Cemetery where 36 soldiers were buried in the aftermath of battle. Their bodies were later interned near San Francisco at the Presidio. Although costly in terms of dollars, the highest toll of this war (or any) was its loss in human life, always, an irreplaceable resource.

All photos by Joe Kraus

The path led us through arid sandhills covered with black pine, without water or grass for five miles. Then from the overlooking higher ground our eyes sighted a yellow expanse of prairie that looked like a wheat field of several 1,000 acres in the waste of sand and pine. . . It was nearly dry with the exception of the clear streams with white sandy bottoms that meandered through it and meet at the eastern end and flowed toward the Deschutes in a very considerable stream.

He was describing an idyllic meadow known as Crane Prairie, a spot which became one of Waldo's favorite areas to camp.

Waldo probably knew the High Cascades better than anyone. He climbed all the major peaks, traced the headwaters of many streams and rivers, measured the depth of lakes, the temperature of hotsprings and made a record of the various native plant life. He also was a great publicist of the beauty and grandeur of the Cascades, calling Odell Lake, for instance, *"one of the fairest of the Cascades' liquid eyes."*

Waldo was a man who had found his Shangra-la, spending the last 27 summers of his life tromping around places like Belknap Springs, Hensleys Meadows and Lake-of-the-Woods. And one of the last entries in his diary in 1907 still showed him to be an unwavering advocate of wilderness preservation.

"The high wild hills about here, totally unfenced and uncultivated are good for eyes that would not have the world altogether cut up into cabbage patches," he wrote from Pamelia Lake.

What would the bearded judge think of his beloved High Cascades today? The grizzly bear and wolf are extinct in Oregon. Crane Prairie lies flooded beneath a 3500 acre reservoir. And a caravan of logging trucks now rumble by some of his treasured campsites.

Yet Waldo would be pleased to know that portions of the High Cascades have been saved — parts of Mount Hood, The Three Sisters, Mount Jefferson, Mount Washington, Diamond Peak, Mount Thielsen and Waldo Lake have all been congressionally protected, their wilderness charm left intact.

All these wildernesses are in a way a tribute to Waldo, champion of those high, lonely places left "undisturbed by human depredation."

day. But at dusk when the results were tabulated it was more bad news. The troops had lost over one-fourth of their men either killed or wounded. That alone was bad enough. What was worse, however, was that throughout the whole long day the troopers never saw one Indian.

When the news reached Army headquarters General E.R.S. Canby was sent out to take charge. But a few months later, still in the midst of defeat and during a peace parley, Canby himself was killed.

Canby's Cross marks the spot where General Canby and the Reverand Eleaser Thomas were attacked and killed during peace negotiations. Also left for dead, A.D. Meacham later recovered.

Revenge was the word then as Colonel Alvin Gillem took command. The Army tried everything in the book. In a last ditch effort they even imported a set of mortars and bombarded the stronghold daily.

The damage these mortars did, however, was not due to the Army's good aim, but to the Indians strange curiosity. When one of the shells landed and failed to explode, a group of Indians gathered around the object to examine it. Several antics were attempted with the device. The Indians curiosity, however, was soon over when a warrier tried to draw the fuze plug out with his teeth.

Despite this, one defeat after another plagued the Army in their plight. But they were never to give up.

Supplied by the latest weapons, replacements, but probably most of all—sheer determination, they were soon to find success. The Modocs were finally forced to abandon their stronghold.

When Captain Jack gave himself up he walked out to an open area and stood in front of the soldiers. He held out his hands and then gazed about him to the land he loved and for which he fought so valiantly. All he said was, "My legs have given out."

The Modoc War was ended. In it the whites had lost eight officers, 39 enlisted men, 16 citizens and two scouts. There were 67 wounded. The Indians lost only five warriors, two of these by their own curiosity over an unexploded mortar shell. The cost to the United States was over a half million dollars. The reservation at Lost River that the Modocs asked for and which would have prevented the war had the whites offered it, was valued at just $10,000.

Today within the old battlefield the National Park Service has provided good footpaths and well documented markers at each point of interest. Even for a person not versed in western Americana it is not difficult to visualize the struggle that took place.

Visitors, if they look hard, will still find pieces of lead lodged in the hardened lava. And with a little imagination it wouldn't be difficult to see the heads of Indians bobbing up behind the rocks or hear the fire of rifles, the sound of war hoops and Indian drums.

On the trail you can visit the actual cave where Captain Jack and his family lived as well as the rostrum where the Indians discussed peace proposals and plans of attack. You can also see the camping area which the army men used to stake out their tents.

Although the battle at Captain Jack's Stronghold ended in success for the United States Army, old dusty journals in the Pentagon are filled with lessons which were learned there.

Feelings ran high on both sides. The Indians, seeing their homes and their lives torn apart by the whites, reacted as many would today in a similar situation. The whites, threatened as they were by what they imagined as uncontrolled actions of the Indians, also were concerned. They acted at the time as many might today, right or wrong.

With this in mind historians might take to heart the words of Robert Emmet who wrote, "Let not my epitaph be written till other times and other men can do me justice."

No. 44

Prineville's Little Railway

By David Braly

While morning mist still hangs over Ochoco Creek, a train rumbles down the tracks beside it. The whistle blows over and over as the orange cars move slowly east towards a sawmill and waiting lumber.

It is like that every weekday morning in Prineville, and has been like that for a half century. It is the mill that is a half century old; the railroad is older.

The railroad is owned by the city of Prineville itself. It was built by the city many years ago in a way that typifies what we call "the pioneer spirit." The City of Prineville Railway itself is not typical of anything. In a report issued in 1985, the Interstate Commerce Commission called it "the only example in the United States of a railroad which was developed and has been wholly-owned and operated

over a substantial period of time by a municipality."

It all began shortly after the turn of the century, when the presence of a railroad could mean prosperity to a town or region, and the absence of one could mean extinction.

In those days, there was only one big town in Central Oregon: Prineville. Bend was one among dozens of small villages. Others included Powell Butte, Paulina, Sisters, Willoughby, Ochoco, Terrebonne and La Monta. Redmond and Madras did not exist.

Prineville was a cattle town of about a thousand people. Located on the banks of Crooked River and Ochoco Creek beneath ancient rimrocks, it was a green oasis in a land of sagebrush and juniper. Farmers and ranchers from a hundred miles in every direction went to Prineville for their

supplies and their entertainment. It was the seat of Crook County, which then covered all of Central Oregon, and the location of the only high school in the region.

All that Prineville lacked to secure its future was a railroad. There were many schemes to attract one, but nothing ever came of them. All anyone could do was wait and hope that eventually some railroad mogul would take an interest in Central Oregon.

Eventually one did: James J. Hill.

Hill decided to build a railroad into Central Oregon, but not to Prineville. Hill's worst enemy was Edward H. Harriman. Harriman had a virtual monopoly on transportation in California. Hill decided that the way to break that monopoly was by penetrating California from the north, and the best way to do that was to build a

railroad from the Columbia straight down into California. Prineville was not on the straight line between those two points. Bend was. Hill built towards Bend.

Harriman's people tried to stop Hill by building their own railroad along the same route, on the other side of the Deschutes River. As a consequence, Bend soon had two railroads heading towards it, while Prineville had none. The contest was America's last great railroad war, complete with men being beaten, drugged, shot at and ducking boulders dynamited on them by their rivals. Finally, a compromise was reached, and it was only one railroad that reached Bend in October 1911. That was enough.

Bend prospered. Bend boomed. In fact, Bend became the fastest booming town in America for the 1910-20 decade.

For Prineville, the railroad was disastrous. The economy hit the skids, businesses failed and people left the area for greener pastures. Everyone kept saying, "If only we could get a railroad in here . . ."

After the failure of numerous efforts to attract railroads, it was suggested at a city council meeting in February 1916, that the city itself build a railroad from Prineville to the main line, 19 miles away.

By a 358-1 vote, Prineville's citizens endorsed the plan. Although the projected cost was a whopping $100,000, they believed that it was the only way to save the town from extinction.

Despite volunteer labor, despite food and wagons provided free by farmers, war prices forced the construction costs above $300,000. Enthusiasm for the project declined, but workers continued building the tracks.

The 19 miles of rail were laid from Prineville to a place on the main line ever after known as Prineville Junction, near Redmond. Depots were built in both Prineville and Prineville Junction. An office, shop and cattle pens were built at the Prineville depot, a tall, single-story building on North Main Street. Sidings were constructed at O'Neil and Wilton, hamlets west of town.

Both freight and passenger service were underway by 1919.

Prineville celebrated.

But the railway barely survived infancy. After the war, the popularity of motor transportation cut passenger use so badly that it was eventually dropped. Freight use was halved by the Depression. The railway would have gone bankrupt if it had been privately owned. The city at one time was in default on interest of $120,000 on a $385,000 bond debt incurred for the railway. But the city continued to

OPPOSITE: The Galloping Goose, Prineville's first engine. Started in 1916 with an estimated cost of $100,000, the project took three years and an additional $200,000 to complete.

TOP: With the advent of the automobile, passenger service declined but eventually sawmills in the area provided the railway with steady, profitable business. Shown here is the old coal burning locomotive.

MIDDLE: Prineville Junction in the early days.

This remains the western terminus of the city owned railway and from here rail cars carrying freight are put onto Burlington Northern and Union Pacific tracks.

ABOVE: A modern diesel engine has replaced the early work horses of the Prineville railway. Lumber continues to be the major outbound freight but most of the line's income is derived from inbound loads of tires headed for a large tire distributorship in Prineville.

Photos Courtesy of Crook County Historical Society

back the railway, confident that some-day sawmills would be built in Prine-ville to tap the area's timber, which included the largest stand of Ponderosa pine in America.

And mills did come eventually. Ochoco Lumber Co. and Alexander-Yawkey Lumber Co. moved into Prineville in 1938. The Hudspeth family, operating in adjoining Wheeler County, began shipping lumber out by the little railway after first trucking it into Prineville. Eventually, the Hudspeths moved into Prineville, where they established several mills and became the largest producer of yellow pine in the United States.

The big mills saved the little railroad.

Indeed, when the railroad was falling apart because of lack of mainten-ance, it was the mills which rescued it. They needed the railroad as much as the railroad needed them. In 1946, the mills loaned the city money for the construction of new tracks of heavi-er rail. They also insisted upon hiring a professional railroad man as man-ager, C. C. McGlenn.

The railroad turned a profit in 1946 and continued to do so for the next thirty years.

Although the principal function of the railroad has been to give the mills a means of transporting their goods to market — thereby securing jobs for townspeople — dividends from the City of Prineville Railway have had many other benefits also.

For many years, Prineville called itself "The City of No City Taxes." It was the only incorporated town in the United States that collected no taxes. The railway paid all costs of city government.

The railway paid — totally or in part — for a lot of other things in Prineville, too. City Hall, for example, was built with railroad money. Rail-road money also went into a modern street lighting system, the city swim-ming pool, a modern sewage disposal system, park and recreation facilities and the high quality paving of almost all of Prineville's streets. The ICC report said this latter cost was especial-ly expensive because of the unusual width of Prineville's streets.

Early in 1986, the Prineville Railway loaned a private company $100,000 to build a new moulding mill in Prineville. Only access to railway funds allowed the city of 5800 to swing such a deal, which has so far brought more than a dozen new jobs to the community.

Unfortunately, while the railway was paying for so many city improve-ments during the 'sixties and early 'seventies, too little money was being retained for upgrading the railway tracks and equipment. Although they were in better shape than after World War II, the tracks were coming apart. An intense effort has gone into rebuild-ing them during the last half dozen years, aided by about $2 million in grants from the Federal Railroad Ad-ministration.

Today, the City of Prineville Rail-way is headquartered in a small depot on North Main, a modern building that little resembles the first depot that was the center of many commu-nity activities. A roundhouse is located just west, across North Main and up the tracks a few hundred feet. The railway employs about twenty people.

Every day, the orange train rumbles out of Prineville, crisscrossing Ochoco Creek and Crooked River, under the long, flat rimrocks, past the ranches and farms, to Prineville Junction, where the cars will be put onto Burling-ton Northern and Union Pacific tracks. Lumber remains the main outbound traffic, although most of the railway's revenue comes from inbound ship-ments of tires headed for the Les Schwab Company of Prineville, the largest independent tire company in America.

Even today, not all is peaceful with the railway. Excluding the federal grants for new rail construction, the City of Prineville Railway lost $209,790.51 during 1980-84 inclusive, and the forecast for the future is for more losses. The railway's manager threw the town into turmoil in 1984 when he tried to branch out into the trucking business in competition with local private trucking firms, and then the city council's commission that oversees the railway tried to conceal the particulars of the venture by declar-ing that it was not subject to state records and meetings laws. These ac-tions prompted the truckers and the Bend *Bulletin* to sue the commission, costing the city over $25,000 in legal and other expenses. The commission lost in court.

But it is likely that the railway will survive the losses and the contro-versies which have plagued it in recent years. It has weathered many severe storms. Besides, the shippers — Les Schwab and Prineville's eight mills — need the railway. So too, do the 2000 people who work for those shippers.

Today, as a half century ago, the little railway is what keeps the little town alive, and *vice versa*.

The big mills saved the little railroad. Indeed, when the railroad was falling apart because of lack of maintenance, it was the mills which rescued it. They needed the railroad as much as the railroad needed them.

Frontier Tycoon

By David Braly

People entering Central Oregon today enjoy what they call "the pleasures of travel." They look out upon rich green forests and snow-capped mountains from the comfort of their air-conditioned car or truck or bus or airplane and wish that they had more time for this sort of thing.

But let us return for a moment to the time when Shaniko was the end of the line and Mack Cornett was the king of transportation.

Although it is now a ghost town, at the turn of the century Shaniko was the bustling distribution center for Central Oregon. People and merchandise reached the end of the rails there and other modes of transportation had to be utilized to reach their final destinations. Freight wagons carried the merchandise. The people — unless they had brought along a horse or were willing to walk a hundred or more miles — took a stagecoach.

The chances are excellent that the stagecoach they took belonged to Mack Cornett. He owned most of them. In fact, Cornett was the sole proprietor of the longest stage line under one management in the United States.

The life of George McIntire Cornett is one of those rags-to-riches sagas which are frequently heard about and seldom experienced first hand.

Mack Cornett was still a youth when he traveled to Oregon. At the age of 22 he was herding sheep in the John Day hills. He worked as a hand on several Central Oregon ranches before he bought his first stagecoach

in 1886.

Cornett was a hard worker and all business. He operated the 200-mile-long route between Shaniko and Silver Lake, the longest continuous line in the United States. He had to drive over roads unworthy of being called trails atop a small coach that bumped across rocks, brush, and soil cracks behind horses who kicked up dust aplenty, and had to do it regardless of whether it was a hundred degrees or ten.

He prospered.

Cornett bought more horses, more stages, and hired more drivers. He became the principal stage operator in the region.

He headquartered his business in

Prineville, where he was stage agent and had a small two-story house. With a population of one thousand, Prineville was the big town of Central Oregon and the seat of Crook County, which included the modern counties of Crook, Deschutes, and Jefferson.

He married Effie Blanche Toney in January 1893. His bride was the daughter and granddaughter of Methodist circuit riders. They eventually had four daughters, although one died when she was 18.

Meanwhile, Cornett was promoting new lines and expanding his business interests. He built a road between Shaniko and Prineville for his coaches. He also established a line that was even longer than the one from Shaniko to Silver Lake. This one ran from Shaniko to Burns.

Soon, more than 500 miles of stage lines emanated from Prineville. They ran to Shaniko, Burns, Sisters, Crook, La Monta, Mitchell, and Bend. Cornett's coaches left and entered Prineville continually, and even the little hamlet of Sisters was visited by a Cornett stagecoach from Prineville every afternoon. At first Cornett used White Steamers. Later he bought E.M.F. stages, and still later Chalmers, Studebakers, and other cars. Eventually he owned more than a hundred vehicles and 360 stage horses. Teams of these horses were kept at stations along the routes so that drivers could change horses quickly. Horses were still used during bad weather after motor vehicles had replaced most stagecoaches.

Winning the U.S. mail contract

helped make the Cornett lines profitable. All the mail for Central Oregon as far south as Burns was sent by train to Shaniko, then reloaded onto a Cornett stagecoach bound for Prineville. Cornett's men took the mail bags to the Prineville Post Office, where the letters and packages were sorted and then put back onto Cornett stages headed for the towns and villages designated on the addresses.

Cornett now employed dozens of men. His stage lines had 26 offices. He bought ranches to grow hay and grain for the stage horses. He branched out into farming. Cornett also acquired interests in mercantile establishments.

Many of Cornett's drivers were brought north from his native Kentucky. Among the best known drivers was Jim Toney, of Mrs. Cornett's family. Another, on the Mitchell, Paulina, and Bear Creek run, was Lyle Hibbard, a brother of Mack's niece-in-law. Hibbard later ran sheep for Cornett. Clark Ewing was on the Burns run. Other well-known drivers included Grover Ewing, Scotty Scott, Walter Cheek, Harry Adams, W.E. Claypool, Chester Hollingshead, John Hunsaker, Dick Hoffner, Walt Vandervert, Aaron Pike, and John, Joe, and Tom Sumner. Perhaps the best known of all Cornett drivers was the colorful Kentuck Ledford. Ledford married Miss Jennie Williamson, a daughter of Congressman J.N. Williamson, and was appointed Prineville postmaster.

Members of Cornett's family also came north. His nephew John Cornett worked for him briefly in 1909, then returned to Kentucky. When he reappeared in Crook County several years later he was accompanied by his bride, and this time he stayed. Another nephew, Levi "Boss" Cornett, was not employed by Mack but managed to build up a large ranch west of Prineville. Mack's sister Julia McDaniel arrived with six daughters after her husband died in 1901. Mack helped her and the older girls find jobs.

Cornett became one of Central Oregon's most prominent citizens. His ranch holdings were sufficiently large that the local newspaper referred to him as a "cattle baron." Its editor quizzed him about economic conditions in a foreign country he had just visited. He was also appointed to the vice presidency of the Crook County Bank.

Although Cornett remained a man of simple tastes (his recreation consisted of motoring, swimming, and fishing with his daughters), in 1911 he built a new house in Prineville at 331 West First Street that can only be described as grandiose in a dusty little cow town. Three stories high, with a basement besides, it contained a reception hall, paneled buttressed stairway, 32x15 living room, 22x14 dining room, brick fireplace with tile hearth, plate-glass mirrors, and a basement washroom and laundry. The second floor had a bath, toilet and lavatory. The bathroom was enameled, but everything else was covered with select flat grain fir and stained in golden and Flemish oak. It was steam heated. The house cost Cornett between six and ten thousand dollars.

He could afford this extravagance. His businesses continued to prosper. By 1913, he had 13 automobiles operating on his stage routes. He was among the first stage operators to use automobiles. Cornett's cars traveling over rough Central Oregon routes served as a testing ground for Detroit automakers, who were kept informed of breakdowns and other problems with their products. Cornett bought his first truck about 1916.

A Prineville newspaper article in August 1918 said of Cornett: "Large farming operations, particularily in the management of Cornett & Company Mercantile establishment, in this city and vice presidency of the Crook County Bank has interested him since his retirement from the stage business on the coming of the railroads and automobile stage lines."

It is unclear exactly when he ceased operating the lines, although it appears to have been sometime between 1916 and 1918. Events were moving fast for Central Oregon transportation during these years, with the arrival of the railroad at Bend and the preparations in Prineville to build a municipally-owned railroad to the main line. Cornett's wife died in 1917, which may or may not have been a factor. Mack's nephew John Cornett assumed the management of the lines after his retirement.

But retirement from the stage business did not mean retirement from all business. In March 1920, Cornett bought a sawmill on McKay Creek. He relocated the mill on Grizzly Mountain, northwest of Prineville, where a timber supply was available. This business, the Cornett & Maison Lumber Company, hauled milled lumber down to Prineville, then shipped it out over the newly-built City of Prineville Railway. The first shipment in June 1920 went to Mexico.

Cornett took his share of losses, though. In 1907, G.N. Clifton and he had established a general mercantile under the name of Clifton & Cornett. Cornett bought out Clifton in 1916, continuing the business as Cornett & Company. When the Ochoco National Forest was formed its officials established their office in the big, roomy Cornett store. However, on June 1, 1922, a fire destroyed two city blocks in Prineville, causing $350,000 worth of damage. Twenty businessmen were put out of business. The Cornett store was totally wiped out, and the Forest Service lost its office there and its records.

Cornett rebuilt, but he never re-entered the retail business. He rented

Continued on Page 52

OPPOSITE TOP: The old Heisler Stage Stop. Passengers include "Mack" Cornett, his wife Effie and two daughters Zuela and Zoe.
OPPOSITE BOTTOM: Prominent Prineville citizens near the turn of the century. Front row: Granville Clifton and Charles Dinwiddie. Back row: Warren Crooks, "Mack" Cornett and George Reams
RIGHT: Cornett's house in Prineville as it stands today.
    Photos Courtesy Crook County Historical Society

THE SECRET OF THE

By Mike Mitchell

The ambiance is definitely "Wild West" or perhaps "Early Klondike." It is available to all on a first-come, first-served basis and there is no fee for its use. All that is asked is that guests leave the cabin clean and a supply of firewood. There is good, fresh water from the creek in front of the cabin and an outhouse is located approximately 50 yards to the north. Fishing is good for brook trout up to 15 inches in both the creek and lake.

Sound too good to be true? It's not. But it is one of a kind. It's the last cabin in the Three Sisters Wilderness.

Hikers stop from time to time to spend a night or two. Now and then a trapper will winter there trapping for mink and marten. But other than the "Friends of Muskrat," the loosely knit organization which cares for the cabin, few know the intriguing story of the man who built it. Fewer still know the cabin's secret.

It was built in 1934 by Luther Metke, Allen Bishop and a couple of helpers. Ted Wallace of Fall River hired them to build it for $250 to serve his muskrat farm. It failed because the mink and marten killed the muskrats Wallace had released.

Although the muskrat farm was a failure, the cabin has been a resounding success with every hiker or horsepacker who spent a night there. It is an authentic 1930's trapper cabin located in the Three Sisters Wilderness. It comes complete with an old fashioned wood cookstove, a wood heating stove, two beds, table and chairs, cupboards, pots and pans, and usually a supply of food and firewood others have thoughtfully left.

The secret of the cabin at Muskrat Lake isn't its location, although it is remote. Nor is it its builder, Luther Metke, who was well known. The biographical film, "Luther Metke at 94" was nominated for an academy award in 1980. The secret is a combination of knowledge, putting the man, the cabin and the location together.

Luther Metke, logger, philosopher, poet, homesteader, early labor organizer and, particularly, a builder of log cabins, was born February 20, 1885 in Buffalo, New York. He spent his early years in Minnesota and at the age of

15 enlisted in the navy. He was fond of telling stories of adventure in China when he sailed up the Yangtze River to Peking and of battles in the Spanish-American War.

He returned from the Philippines on the battleship Oregon. In 1907 he homesteaded at the present site of the multimillion dollar resort, Sunriver. Here he built a cabin, which in 1912, he began sharing with his bride, the former Anna Dobbs, who had come to America at the age of 16 from Ireland.

When logging fell off in the 1920s, Metke sold out and moved to Bend, where he and Bob Decourcey built and operated Bend Troy Laundry. In 1940, he moved to Camp Sherman, where in 1977 at the age of 92, he started his last log cabin. He finished it when he was 94. In 1983, he was grand marshal of Bend's Christmas Parade and over 200 people attended his 100th birthday February 20, 1985 in Camp Sherman. He was Oregon's last surviving veteran of the Spanish-American War. He died April 7, 1985 at St. Charles Medical Center in Bend.

This writer never met Luther Metke. The biographical facts were gleaned

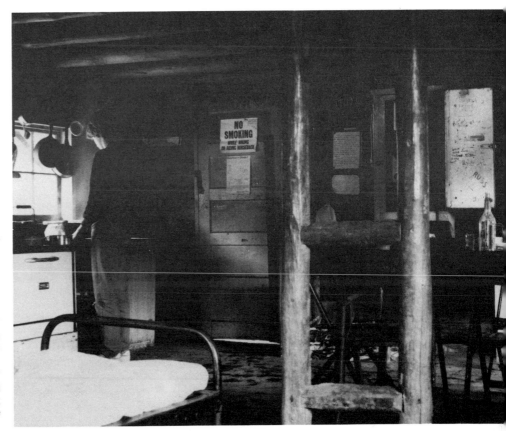

OPPOSITE: The cabin built by Luther Metke and Allen Bishop in 1934 to support a muskrat farm envisioned by Ted Wallace. The muskrat farm failed but the cabin still stands along the shore of Muskrat Lake.   Mike Mitchell Photo

ABOVE: The back door of the cabin facing Muskrat Lake. In the past the lake has risen enough to flood the cabin floor.
        Photo courtesy of Deschutes Historical Society

RIGHT: The author's son inside the cabin. Graffiti on the walls tell tales of previous visits to the lake; a distructive practice that is frowned upon if the cabin is to survive for others to enjoy.
        Mike Mitchell Photo

TOUCH OF HISTORY
Continued from Page 55

the meandering river, the mountains, the flights of ducks and geese, and the passing parade of people in Drake Park.

Ruth Caldwell Coyner died in 1980; W.C. Coyner died in 1981. In his wallet were found pictures of his beloved point. Some were newspaper clippings. Some were photographs. All showed the point abounding with greenery, the efforts of nearly 40 years of love.

The point property was willed to the Coyners' surviving sons and grandchildren. Faced with burdensome inheritance taxes, they are forced to sell. The property sale, handled exclusively by Julie Fenton Young of Steve Scott and Company, is creating interest among buyers up and down the coast. It has even been considered by one Hollywood film company as a location site.

Yet the prospect of the sale is causing concern for the Coyner heirs. "I know my father would have never wanted us to sell the point," says Craig C. Coyner, the eldest son of W.C. and Ruth, "but we are without another choice in the matter. Our hope is that whoever buys the point keeps the property in one piece for visual and historical reasons. We also pray that the new owner gives the land as much love as my father did."

FRONTIER TYCOON
Continued from Page 49

his new building to the Forest Service, Post Office, and several mercantile establishments.

He still had his vast holdings of land laden with sheep and the bank. At least he had the bank until two days before Christmas in 1926. In the midst of an agricultural depression, the Crook County Bank closed its doors forever that day.

That was the year he remarried, to Mrs. Josephine Taylor. His daughters had now grown and they too married. They moved away from Prineville.

Mack Cornett died May 20, 1932.

In 1940 the Cornett house was converted into a hospital. Today it's a boarding house. A large building he had constructed in Paulina to store freight and serve as a post office also remains. It's now the Paulina Store. Little else survives as a legacy of Mack Cornett. No business remains that bears his name. No street name or other public monument recalls him to mind.

A hundred years after an uneducated Kentucky sheepherder bought a stagecoach, the man who built Central Oregon's largest transportation empire is virtually forgotten.

during a quiet afternoon of research at the Deschutes Historical Society in Bend. But one can get a feel for the man and the times he lived in at his cabin.

After the supper dishes have all been done, the children put to bed and the candle light is softly flickering on the cabin walls, let your mind go back to Luther Metke and how he loved and sweated over this cabin during the months of September and October 1934. Examine the finely crafted log walls and think how, after Ted Wallace abandoned the place because all his muskrats were killed by mink, Luther Metke saw opportunity. He spent the entire winter of 1935 here —trapping mink.

Take a walk outside the cabin into the starry night. Enjoy the peace and timelessness of the setting and think of the young Metke steaming up the Yangtze to the seat of the imperial Manchu dynasty.

Finally, take some time to read the graffiti on the walls, a practice this writer usually abhores. But you should read about the man who came to the cabin one spring and found it occupied by a bear. Or read about the fellow who got flooded out late one Christmas night when the lake rose. Read about the love people have had for this old cabin over the years and think about the Metke poem,

"It isn't what we have
It isn't what we know
The only thing that matters
Is the 'good will' deeds we sow."

If you do this, you may get a feel for Luther and his times. The past and the present have a way of coming together up there. That's the real secret of the log cabin at Muskrat Lake.

To get to the cabin, take the Cascade Lakes Highway to Big Cultus Lake about 40 miles southwest of Bend. Follow the signs on the paved road to the campgrounds. The last ½ mile is gravel. You will see a sign pointing to the Winopee trailhead to the right. Take this good dirt road the last 200 yards to the trailhead. From here it is 5½ miles over the well marked and maintained Winopee trail to Muskrat Lake. After 3½ miles, a sign points to the right, north, to Winopee Lake. Head north on this mostly level trail another 2 miles to Muskrat Lake. The trail passes within 50 feet of the cabin which is in an open meadow on the north shore of the lake. There is a bridge in front of the cabin over the creek. Knock on the door and if it's vacant, it's yours.

A Touch of History in Downtown Bend

By Bob Woodward

Travelling east or west, pioneer wagon trains arrived at a bend where they caught their last glimpse of the Deschutes River. Knowing that once the river had been forded arduous mountain and desert travel lay ahead, they affectionately named the bend in the river "farewell bend".

Up river a short distance lay another bend in the river that would become a more prominent point in years to come. This land is currently known as Coyner Point and protrudes out into Mirror Pond, directly across from Drake Park.

What we see today differs somewhat from the pioneer's view of the point. The sisters remain the same — snowcapped and glittering. While we see the green of Drake Park, the pioneer traveler saw a bank covered with scrawny trees and scrub brush. On the opposite side of the river, modern day viewers most often recall the bright green summer or golden autumn leaves that cascade down from stately Willows on Coyner Point. A hundred years ago that point was marshy bottom land hardly suitable for anything but marsh life.

Times change, and as the town called Farewell Bend grew along the banks of the Deschutes, so the scenery changed. Coyner Point in particular underwent a dramatic change during the past sixty-four years thanks mainly to the efforts of the various families who owned and cared for the property during that period.

The history of the point is inextricably tied in with the history of Bend. Shortly after the town name was cut down to Bend by federal postal officals, a sawmill operated downstream from the point. The old river ford fell into disuse as bridges spanned the Deschutes in several

sites. In 1909, the Bend Water, Light and Power Company built a dam just below the point. This dam backed the Deschutes up to form Mirror Pond.

With the creation of the pond, property on both sides of the river became most valuable. No piece was more sought after than the point which would first become known as Hosch Point and then by its current name — Coyner Point.

In 1918, J.F. Hosch, a physician, state legislator and Bend's first mayor, started the transformation of the point from swampland into a lush garden spot with the construction of his house on the point's high ground.

Hosch built his English style cottage to best take advantage of the

The once rushing waters of the Deschutes River swirl around the point...known today as Coyner Point. This photo was taken in 1905 from the Drake residence. Oregon Historical Society Photo

Aerial view of Bend's Deschutes River winding around Coyner Point, taken during the mid '70s. Oregon Historical Society Photo

Inset Photo: The "point" after the Deschutes was dammed to form Mirror Pond. A few houses and foot bridge are visible. Oregon Historical Society Photo — Boychuck Collection.

breathtaking views from the point. The spacious living room was so designed that the windows looked out to Drake Park on one side and toward the Sisters on another side. From the master bedroom, complete with fireplace, and the connected sleeping porch, the Sisters were also visible.

Upon completion of the house, Hosch began his land reclamation.

Fill was needed for the swampy bottom land and by trading medical services for wagon loads of rock, Hosch soon filled in the marshy portion of the point. The lava rock walls visible today along the point are the result of Hosch's bartering.

As the land was filled, the doctor began to import and plant trees of all descriptions around the property.

This was the beginning of the point's significance as a horticulturalist's paradise. Even today, experts have trouble identifying some of the evergreen varieties dotting the property.

After Hosch's death in the late 1930's, the point was purchased by another state legislator, Vernon Forbes. Forbes' contribution to the history of the point came mostly in the form of his wife's lavish purchases for the interior of the house. Oriental rugs, antiques, and art pieces filled the rooms. They remained with the house when it was sold along with the point property in 1943 for $17,000.

The purchaser was William Craig Coyner, a native Iowan who had been raised in Oklahoma. In 1914, Coyner went west to seek his fortune. He settled in Crescent, eventually moving on to Bend where he met and married Ruth Caldwell.

Ruth Caldwell had arrived in Bend in 1905 following a wagon trip over the Cascades from Albany, Oregon with her parents. She was the first woman hired by the Shevlin-Hixson Lumber Company (Diamond International) and in her later years was Bend's leading music teacher and a prominent clubwoman.

W.C. Coyner was a financial jack of all trades. He opened the first collection agency in the Bend area and was an early property developer.

But it was apparent to all who knew "W.C." well that his first love was the point property. He cared for the land like a child. From the time he and his wife moved onto the point until their deaths during the past two years, the Coyners put all their spare time into landscaping the point.

Shortly after buying the point, W.C. set out to cover Hosch's bartered rock fill with topsoil. And when the final truckload of soil had been dumped and smoothed, 18 inches of topsoil lay over the low section of Coyner Point. Into that soil went grass seeds and thousands of plantings of common and unusual flora.

Enamored of Cushion Mums,

W.C. Coyner, known at "The Chrysanthemum King", laboring over his unusual array of flora, in the fall of 1980.

Coyner crossbred many forms. He would become known during his lifetime as "The Chrysanthemum King".

Mr. Coyner discovered that the point has its own micro climate that allows for very early and late growing seasons. Modified by the proximity to the water and the fact that the point basks in sunlight from just after sunup to sundown year round, Coyner was able to make things grow that had never before or since been able to survive in the high desert country.

Stricken by a coronary attack in 1962, Mr. Coyner curtailed his active business life. The attack did not, however, limit his gardening time. For the last 20 years of his life, he planted and nurtured the point's trees and flowers.

He added and built. Two rooms went onto the house, a pond was dug at the apex of the point and he created a stone alcove where he could rest and enjoy the Sisters in the distance. Today a well worn bench in the heart of the alcove attests to the many hours Mr. Coyner passed watching Continued on Page 52

A modern day Drake Park with its myriad of activites finds boys fishing, children feeding the ducks, picnicing and canoeing. On the opposite side of Mirror Pond (Deschutes River) lies Coyner Point and its' weeping willows. Oregon State Highway Photo

One Hale

Midvale, Idaho

In the first quarter of the twentieth century, when most people considered the West to have been 'won', a hardy little family fought for survival just north of the Wieser foothills in Idaho. Their name was Hale. Their enemy was not Indian or animal, but too little water and too much cold weather. For they were farmers. Because the Hales couldn't even pry enough wheat from the stingy ground to seed the next year's crop, they once again pulled up their stakes and set off in a covered wagon — Medford, Oregon was their destination.

Only nine years before, in 1912, had the Hales moved from Illinois, choosing the Idaho hills as their home. Their crop would be wheat, since dry wheat ranching purportedly would work well in an area such as Southwestern Idaho. The theory was that the cultivator would till all of his fields, but only plant in half of them, leaving the remainder to fallow. The next year, then, he would alternate. But determination was not enough, and Orlie Hale had to face the fact that the cool, parched sandhills wouldn't cooperate. So when 1921 came he called it quits and decided to head west again.

Once the decision was made, the Hales waited only for May and the spring thaw before they set off, hopes sky high. Bob recalls his excitement, "We'd heard about the fruit orchards in Medford. Picking our own fruit right off the tree. We thought that sure would be something!"

Rumors of vast fruit orchards and temperate winters had already reached them from this small town located near the intersection of the Bear and Rogue Rivers in western Oregon. The valley was said to be loamy and fertile, with the surrounding mountainsides thick in yellow pine, fir, oak, and cedar. It sounded a dream place, almost unreal.

Medford, then, became their goal.

Although Bob remembered seeing a few automobiles on the roads back East in Illinois before his family moved to Midvale, about 30 miles north of the Weiser Sandhills of Idaho, his family was poor and would have to make do with a single covered wagon driven by the family's two horses — Bill, the black, and Dan, the bay. Since it wasn't a large wagon, and most of the room inside would have to go to the ton or so of supplies for the journey, part of the family would have to stay behind. In the end, Volto ('Bob', aged 16), his older brother Orvie ('Buck', 18), 2 sisters Veronica and Mable (14 and 11), and their father Orlie set out. The remainder of the Hale family would wait at the ranch in Midvale: Bob's stepmother Stella and the other half of the Hale children (Geneva, Ray, Vivian, Rosier, and the small grave of little Merrill, who'd died a few years before.) The children were sorry not to be going on the wagon, but they understood that it was too small for all of them. These were children used to hard times, used to living on the edge of poverty. But they weren't poor in family love, and in the West, that was the most prized commodity. There was one more factor, and that was that they knew that soon they would be going to Oregon. To the Hales, as to so many before them, Oregon seemed a paradise.

So they loaded the wagon with flour, dried pork, potatoes, the all important barrel of water, a few tools, a cooking pan or two, and bedding. The wagon also had a 'chamber' inside and a wash tub hung on the back — for watering horses, washing clothes, and bathing. The latter done under duress when visiting a place with plenty of water.

The Hales couldn't afford to get hurt, for they carried no medicines, not even simple aspirins or bandages. Thus it was that on the third day, when Orlie took ill, the only cure was rest — what rest one could get in a bumpily driven wagon. Although they'd averaged about twenty miles a day, the slow, even plodding of the wagon made the younger Hales impatient. Anxious to get there and be done with it, they continually nagged their father, admonishing him to speed it up. When Orlie caught the fever, later diagnosed as a recurrence of the malaria he'd contracted in the Philippines in the Spanish-American War from 1898-99, Bob and Buck eagerly took over. That day, the beleaguered Dan and Bill ran thirty miles.

Pleased with themselves and their accomplishment, the boys settled to sleep on the rough ground with big smiles on their faces. The smiles faded, however, when they awoke the next morning to find the horses stiff and sore. That day the Hales were lucky to cover ten miles.

So the youngsters learned the hard way to relax, to enjoy the journey as

# of a Trail

By July A. Jolly

well as the destination. The days passed and they crossed the Snake River and entered Oregon, walking alongside the crunching iron wheels of the wagon, veering off into the brush of the desert with their 22 pistol, hoping for jack rabbits, rattlers, and coyotes. At night they would stop, light a fire, and cook their simple meal of hard tack, beans, bacon, or potatoes. Then they'd sack out. Not one of them had a sleeping bag. A blanket under the wagon was often their only bed. If they were lucky they'd have a roof over their heads, provided on occasion by an abandoned farm or shack.

Any breakdown had to be fixed by the Hales themselves. As with most of the wagons that crossed the desert, they didn't bring extra parts. The worst calamity would be if a wheel became irreparable. Luckily, the only major breakdown that the Hales faced was when the wagon's campling pole broke, that is the pole that connects the front and rear portions of the wagon together. They, of course, didn't carry an extra, and so had to halt their journey while Orlie hewed one from a small tree before they could continue.

The trail the Hales were to follow

The Hales' long and arduous journey began in Midvale, Idaho, where the family lived from 1912 until 1921 (photo taken in 1920). Lured by the promise of fertile land and mild winters in Medford, Oregon they packed their possessions in a single covered wagon and headed west. The map at right traces their route from Midvale to Bend where the family would remain for ten years.

Photo courtesy of Idaho Historical Society.

from the Snake River across Oregon was known as the Central Oregon Emigrant Trail. First scouted in 1845 by Stephen H.L. Meek, the brother of the more well-known Col. Joe Meek, the central trail was to be a more direct route to the plush Willamette Valley. The original Oregon trail took a sharp northward track once the Snake River was crossed. Stephen Meek didn't. His party plunged straight into the heart of Oregon's harshest desert. Known to its inhabitants as the High Desert, this

arid land was formed by millions of years of lava flows from the growing peaks of the Cascade and Klamath Ranges. layer upon layer of molten lava poured down, erosion took away the weakest portions, mountains blocked the life-giving rain from the west, and the High Desert rose. Confused amid the myriad ridges, canyons, dry lake beds and washes of the unknown desert, the Meek party wandered, lost, for weeks. The water ran out and over seventy people perished before the party reached the

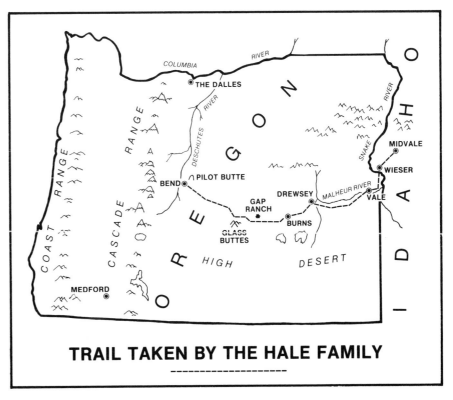

TRAIL TAKEN BY THE HALE FAMILY

ABOVE: A view of the Snake River country along the border between Idaho and Oregon. Rugged, difficult terrain to cross in a covered wagon.
Photo Courtesy of Idaho Historical Society.

BELOW: Retracing the journey of 1921, Bob Hale (R) and his son Don locate a portion of the old trail embedded in stone. Picture taken in 1985.

Deschutes River, where the town of Bend is now situated.

It was this desert that the Hales were to cross alone, in their single-team wagon. Arid, high, almost treeless except for juniper, and chilly cold at night, this desert was to be their challenge. Day in and day out, they passed sage-filled gullies, grassy hills, and buttes thrusting tall and flat-topped like sentinels of the desert. The only evidence of spring was in the purple lupines and yellow-belled flowers that sometimes mixed in with the grasses on the hills. In the distance were dark lines of ridges, promises of things to come. Seventy years later, the area was as wild as when Meek first crossed it. Because even though it was true that homesteaders had come, they had also gone away again, their dreams desiccated by the heartless drought of the region, until the dry husks of their farms littered the trail further westward.

From the border of Idaho, the Hales followed the Malheur River for about the first 60 miles. The Malheur was named by fur trader Peter Ogden in 1826 when his cache of furs and supplies hidden there were rifled by Indians. Furious, he dubbed the place "evil hour" or Malheur. The region, like the rest of the desert, is virtually treeless. But it is hardly flat, dug out by the river and occasional creeks into vast reaches of sage- and juniper-filled folds.

About 6 miles after leaving the Malheur, the Hales crossed into Harney County, the largest county in Oregon, and came upon Drewsy, named for a local rancher's daughter when the original name Gouge Eye (for the common way of dealing with malcontents) found disfavor with postal officers.

Even though the 140 mile trek from Vale, on the Idaho-Oregon border, to Burns took the stage two and a half arduous days of constant travel, changing the horses every fifteen miles, the Hales, walking at a much slower pace and unable to change horses, took longer. To them, the town of Burns, dusty and tiny as it was, seemed like an oasis. Located on the premises of the cattle ranch of Pete Stinger, the formal capital of the old cattle empire was also the home of the Paiute Indian Village, the only independent Indian settlement in Oregon, begun in 1878 after the Bannock War.

After a short rest, the Hales said goodbye to Burns and pressed on across one of the driest portions of the High Desert. One night, about 40 miles west of Burns, they drew in at a place called the Gap Ranch, belonging to M.M. Brown. Much to their pleasure, the boys were invited over to dinner and to spend the night. Bob, a hunter himself now, remembers being impressed by the fact that the man and his wife seemed pretty well-off and had walls filled with game trophies — from rattlers to coyotes to antelope. The next morning, Bob and Buck saw two riders leave the Ranch with heavy jugs hanging from the sides of their saddles and guessed that some of the Gap Ranch's wealth emanated from bootlegged moonshine. It was, after all, the Prohibition. "There was a lot of that going on in those hills," Bob recalls. "That's why we didn't venture too far off the track." It also accounted for some of the rather unfriendly 'greetings' the Hales got as they passed by certain areas.

About twenty to thirty miles west of the Gap Ranch are the Glass Buttes, soaring 2000 feet up. Considered the largest outcropping of iridescent obsidian (lava glass) in the world, they are a source of most western Indians' spear and arrowheads. Some sources say that Indian relics from as far east as Ohio can be traced to these Buttes.

After passing the Glass Buttes, the Hales rode along the Klamath Rim, the great drainage ridge separating the northern and southern portions of Eastern Oregon. The valley formed, called the Imperial Valley, was yet another location where homesteaders gave up thier hopes of turning Eastern Oregon into a great wheat growing area.

It was about this time that the Hales ran into a bit of trouble. Like the Meek party seventy years before, they lost their trail. Then luck shone on them again in the form of a farmhouse. Unlike many they passed, this one seemed occupied. Bob was sent to ask directions. He walked about a quarter of a mile and was almost at the house when suddenly out of the brush burst a tearing, kicking antelope. As Bob watched in horror, it snorted and dashed right at him. Bob took flight and saw a fence. "I don't know if I went under, over, or through that fence, I was so scared," he remembers. His father later told him that before this time he didn't ever think anyone could outrun an antelope. But Bob did, heart thumping and legs pounding, to the door of the house.

It was only later that he was told that the antelope was only playing and was the farmer's pet.

Once on the trail again, the biggest concern became water. At one point their supply of it had gotten so low that there was only one quart left to share between the five people and the horses, which had priority. All along the trip, they'd been buying water from farmers, who charged about 25 cents per horse, as Bob recalls, to let them draw from their wells, some of which plummeted over 1000 feet down. Travelers in the desert can take a lot of hardship, but not lack of water. Luckily, the very next day brought a filled barrel.

With fears subsided, the Hales continued. They were passing through open range now, and Bob remembers seeing thousands of sheep, very few cattle, and "millions of jack rabbits". This was after the great cattle-sheep disputes, and the encroaching sheep had diminished the great cattle empires that used to flourish in the region. He also recalls that there was grass everywhere. He has been back since and cattle once again outnumber sheep and the grass is gone. But in 1921 things were different, no finished roads, very little traffic, and the wide blue sky.

Further along the trail, the Hales stopped at an abandoned shack and set up for the night, Buck and Bob deciding to sleep inside. The next morning, just before dawn, Bob heard a noise and woke to find a large, shadowy figure of a man leaning over him. He wasn't particularly frightened, he says, and soon the man faded. Bob still doesn't know if it was real or a dream.

They continued travelling, crossing a couple of creeks, ever thankful that they had the necessary iron wheels. Wooden wheeled wagons wouldn't have lasted two days out on the desert, because that type of wheel required a daily wetting, according to Bob, to keep from cracking. Extra water for wheels just wasn't feasible.

May melded into June and the Hales crossed a wide, flat expanse known as Dry River. This river dates back to prehistoric times when, although it is hard to imagine, Eastern Oregon was a land of huge lakes. Now, however, Dry River traces a fifty mile path across the region, without a drop of water in sight. Definitely in sight by now, though, were the white cresting peaks to the west: Mount Hood, Mount Jefferson, Broken Top and the Sisters.

After another day's travel the Hales spotted Pilot Butte, an ancient cinder cone towering 511 feet above the desert. This was the landmark used by emigrants back through history to guide them to the place where they could most easily cross the Deschutes River and turn northward toward the Willamette Valley. It was a farewell of sorts to the High Desert, so the pioneers called the place Farewell Bend. Only the latter part of the name remains today.

So they arrived at the joining place of desert and mountain called Bend, Oregon. A logging town, Bend was the largest population the Hales had seen in a month, and it seemed wonderful, bustling, alive. In fact, according to government records, Bend had expanded faster than any other town in the nation between 1910 and 1920, going from 536 persons to 5415 during that decade, a 910 percent increase!

The Hales camped just outside the town and Orlie went in to see if he could get work to earn some money so that they could buy supplies to continue to Medford. One of Bend's two huge sawmills took both Orlie and Buck as employees, but said that Bob was too young and would have to go to school for a year before he could work. "And that wasn't easy, since I hadn't been to school since the eighth grade," Bob says.

After working awhile, the Hales sent back to Midvale for Stella and the rest of the family, who sold everything and came out. By this time the railroads had a train operating to Bend's sawmills from The Dalles, on the Washington-Oregon border. Using earnings made at the mill, the family rode the train along the Deschutes River to Bend, thus reuniting the Hales once more.

As things went, however, it was ten more years before any of the Hales made it to Medford. Bend turned out to be an all right place, according to Bob Hale. He even married there in 1925.

But the trip west over the desert from Idaho would always stay with him. "I'll never forget that trip. That father of mine had to have a lot of nerve to take off like he did," Bob says. Indeed he did. Men like Hale and families like the Hales are why we have an America as great as it is.

Dust, Jacks & Matrimony Vines

By Michael Forrest

(Oregon Homesteading 1910-1914)

"**I**t is totally out of the question." Her green eyes burning with anger, Adelaide McMains wasn't about to let her youngest son and last remaining child go any further west than their large and comfortable home in Colorado Springs, Colorado. The year was 1909 and Leon, the son who had just defied his mother for the first time in his life, had reached the age of twenty-one. His father, William, a bit of a wanderlust and adventurer, who had been estranged from his wife for several years, wrote to Leon from San Francisco to congratulate him on his coming of age and to make him a proposition. "The Homestead Law has been amended," he eagerly wrote, "and now the government will give, for the asking, 320 beautiful Oregon state acres to any adult, and all he has to do is to live there for a few years. There is certain to be great interest in this offer and I think you and I should take advantage of it as soon as possible. Just think, Leon," he enthused, "640 acres for the two of us; that is one square mile of land!"

What William failed to tell his son, however, even if he had bothered to read the fine print of the homestead advertisements which appeared in most of the leading newspapers, was the cold fact that the 320 acres was not a piece of dense forests, lush green meadows and sparkling blue pools for which Oregon,

at least *western* Oregon is so justly famous. But the 320 acres were of "nonirrigable, nonmineral and nontimbered land" in the center of the dry, flat, barren and almost uninhabitable eastern Oregon desert. Futhermore, the "few years" amounted to five long, brutal years of which few homesteaders were able to endure.

All of these "facts", however, did not escape Adelaide who in her effort to thwart the enterprise at any cost, scrutinized every bit of information on homesteading in Oregon. Her arguments against such a venture were sound for no two people could have been more unsuited for such an undertaking. Leon's world was one of escorting "Ada" to the theater and

FAR LEFT: Adelaine McMains. Circa 1905.
LEFT: William McMains. Circa 1912.

FAR LEFT: Leon plowing his field. Circa 1911. LEFT: Leon by his cabin with Ginger, Critter and Spunky. Circa 1911.

acting as cohost to her enumerable teas, luncheons and suppers. William, on the other hand, was a gambler, a sophisticate and man about town. Both were slightly scatterbrained and completely impractical. Yet despite Ada's dire predictions and frequent fainting spells at the very mention of Oregon, a date was set and father and son arranged to meet in Lakeview, Oregon, the county seat, in the Spring of 1910.

If they were discouraged when they first saw their new home, they never mentioned it. For William and Leon it was the beginning of a great new adventure and they were determined to make the most of it. William was already established at the Lakeview Hotel when Leon arrived. He had been to the surveyor's office and looked at the maps. It was not encouraging. The best land, near watering holes or at the edge of forests where one might expect ample rainfall, had all been taken. The best areas left seemed to be in the "high desert", in Christmas Valley, near the small town of Cliff, almost one hundred miles north of Lakeview. Here, it was said, the land was not as desolate, not as hot in the summer nor as frigid in the winter as other areas; and, which was probably its greatest asset, it was not as dry and water, that much needed and priceless commodity, stood at only twenty feet down which meant that digging a well was not impractical.

William, realizing that he and his son were entering into an area for which they were illprepared and unknowledgeable, spent his time picking the brains of the locals. He loved to talk to people and he had that sort of warm personality that attracted people to talk to him and answer his many questions. The new homesteaders, he found, were a mixed lot but were generally as ignorant of desert farming as himself. Many were cocky and anticipated no problems. They were the first to fail. Others came with money and felt they would pay others to do their work. They were the next to fail and left with a little less money to worry about. Still others came who had been born and raised on farms. Having an idea of what they were in for, they came with the greatest determination and a few of these managed to survive.

But, of course, it was the old homesteaders, the ones who were making it, who wandered in and out of Lakeview, that William was most eager to meet. They were proud of their success and were eager to set William and his son on the right path. In addition to much good advice, they also made recommendations on what gear to buy such as some expensive items, as a horse and cart, but also included many inexpensive and indispensable gratuitous items that could be used for a variety of purposes. There were, for example, old whiskey barrels, marvelous containers, especially for those precious drops of soft rainwater that sometimes fell on the desert. They could even be used for their original purpose. "Moonshining" was not unknown amongst the homesteaders. Barrels and boxes of all kinds could also be broken up and the wood put to a variety of uses. Cans. especially the large kerosene cans, could be used as pots, pans, measuring cups, etc. The pages from Sears and "Monkey" Wards catalogs could be sometimes read but more often they were used to satisfy many of the paper needs of the household which included a rather rough form of toilet tissue and an unusual form of wall covering. Flour sacks were also one of the basics. Cut up they could serve as dish cloths, towels, curtains, etc. and a homesteader with some seamstressing abilities could easily transform them into soft undergarments and, if the need arose, diapers.

William and Leon always remembered the day they finally left Lakeview en route to their homestead. Bouncing along in their rickety cart, piled high with their gear, led by an old mare they nicknamed "Pokey", for obvious reasons, their enthusiasm was matched by the wonderfully cool, clear morning and the desert itself which had suddenly come alive following a recent Spring shower. Intermingled with the sage brush, and as far as the eye could see, was a profusion of phloxes, larkspurs, evening primroses and other showy blossoms bursting with color and filling the air with delicate perfumes. Also in abundance were the Oregon jack rabbits. They seemed to be everywhere. Occasionally they also saw a deer or antelope and even a wary coyote or bobcat. As they neared the town of Cliff, they could see in the distance Fort Rock, a semi-circular rock formation caused by an ancient collapse of a volcanic cone; it served then, as now, as a predominate landmark in the area.

In 1910 little was known about the amazing history of Fort Rock. However in recent times, Fort Rock and its surrounding area has yielded a great wealth of archaeological artifacts including some seventy-five sagebrush-bark sandals, more than nine thousand years old, and other items and campfire ashes which indicate the presence of Indians in the vicinity more than thirteen thousand years ago. Also in the same area is Fossil Lake where ancient fossils of prehistoric animals never cease to amaze and excite paleontologists.

Cliff, just twenty miles from the homestead, was, in 1910, not exactly a one horse town but it was certainly close to it. It did support a general store, post office, blacksmith shop, a hotel (of sorts) and a saloon which was always a hub of activity. William was set on spending a few days in Cliff even though Leon was just as set on moving on and seeing their spread. William was resolute. He felt that as newcomers to Cliff, they were in a good position to circulate and make friends with their new neighbors. It didn't take long for him to hear about "Doc" Muth, who rarely came to town but was someone William and Leon should visit. As it turned out, Doc Muth was their nearest neighbor, having settled on the adjoining property. Everyone in Cliff agreed that Doc, a homesteader for four years, was a tremendous source of information. He had built himself a cabin and maintained a "workable" and productive farm. No one knew much about him other than the fact that he lived alone, apparently enjoyed such an existence, and had a great command over nature and the elements. The title of "Doc" was probably conferred on him in respect for his age, for he was well into his sixties, and for his abilities as a desert survivor.

On the last evening of their stay in Cliff, Leon met Ginger in the saloon. Abandoned by some retreating homesteader, Ginger was determined to find a new home and in no time was able to win Leon's heart. Ginger, a white and tan mongrel of uncertain age, became the newest member of the family and the next day she joined William, Leon and Pokey on the last few miles to their home. In the next few years, two other wandering mutts, which Leon named "Critter" and "Spunky", also managed to find a home in Leon's camp.

Doc Muth was found to be an agreeable fellow with twinkling blue eyes and a long white beard. His farm consisted of a one room wooden structure with an adjoining tool shed, a well with an attached wind mill and two acres of assorted vegetables. Although he cautioned that he respected the privacy of others and expected others to respect his, Doc proved to be a great help to William and Leon. His advice was taken, usually without question, and he always proved to be accurate.

On one occasion, however, during the first summer, Doc's dire warning

of an impending dust and wind storm was not taken seriously and it almost proved fatal for Leon who was set on going to Cliff that day. It was a deceptively clear and calm morning, but just as soon as Leon reached the half way point, giant black clouds rolled across the desert floor and Leon and Pokey were soon engulfed in swirls of stinging, penetrating, deadly dust and sand. Both horse and man protected themselves as best they could and managed to drag themselves back to the homestead, but Leon learned his lesson. During future storms, he wisely remained indoors. These storms, which could last for days, were perhaps the most depressing aspect of desert living. The continuous howl of the wind, the ominous black sky and the unrelenting dust that crept down the

chimney, sneaked under the window and door frames and managed to get into everything in the house was enough to tax the sanity of any homesteader.

During the first summer, William's cabin was built to be followed the next year by Leon's one room "shanty". The first winter was scarce on snow but terribly frigid with temperatures dropping well below zero for days on end. A pot bellied iron stove, which burned the long lasting juniper logs, kept William's cabin tolerably warm and comfortable during this long period.

William and Leon were no sooner settled, than the Cliff post office was deluged with pastel pink, perfumed letters and assorted boxes. Ada had not forgotten her son and was determined to give him frequent

CLOCKWISE FROM TOP: Doc Muth standing in front of his cabin. Circa 1910. The "Dudes" baseball team (Leon in foreground with Ginger). Circa 1913. Participants in the Jack Rabbit Drive. Circa 1914. (All Photos Courtesy of Michael Forrester).

tastes of the "good life" so he would not become too "uncouth" and "barbarian". Her letters were filled with such newsy items as theater reviews, social happenings and general gossip. Her boxes were filled with such "necessities" as imported chocolates, silk pajamas and even, in one instance, after Leon had written to his mother and told her of completing his well, a case of French champagne "to celebrate" the accomplishment. In mid 1912, Ada sold her house in Colorado Springs and after threatening to come and visit the homestead, which she never did, moved to San Francisco where her other two sons, Warren and Arthur, were living. Warren was at that time engaged to one of the Le Claire sisters, of a prominent and well-to-do family in town, and Arthur, who would tragically and suddenly die of tuberculosis within this year, was an aspiring actor. Ada settled

into a house on Eddy Street, on one of the few blocks of old homes that had not been damaged by the earthquake and fire that devastated San Francisco just six years before. William and Leon came for Arthur's funeral and Ada was shocked at the transformation that had come over Leon in the past two years. He was no longer fashionably thin, pale and slightly amaciated; instead, he was robust, suntanned and bursting with enthusiasm and vitality. William, whom we hadn't seen for over ten years, she felt hadn't changed at all, he was still the same shady character he always was.

Despite the adversities of nature, the homesteaders were a happy and friendly lot and they often gathered together for "socials" which included square dancing, camp fires and baseball games. Leon helped to organize a baseball team in 1913 which he called the "Dudes" and they

often played other nearby teams in the Christmas Valley area. Another unusual event were the jack rabbit drives. The Oregon jack rabbit, more than any other animal or rodent, was a great menace to the homesteaders. At that time there were millions of them roaming the deserts and the wonderful green shoots growing on homesteaders' farms were treats they couldn't resist. One could catch or shoot some of them but there were always many more to take their place. The drives were a combined effort of a hundred or more homesteaders — men, women and children — who gathered together in one area to eliminate as many of the jacks as possible. A chicken wire compound was built into which thousands of jacks were driven and then clubbed to death. In later years, some counties even offered a five cent bounty for each rabbit killed and many homesteaders found they could make a good living eliminating jacks.

It was a hard life for all homesteaders but it was particularly difficult for the women who endeavored, often against great odds, to maintain a comfortable home for her family. Certainly her battle with dust and dirt was neverending and the scarcity of good water for washing did not help matters. There was also the desolation of the desert which probably discouraged the women more than the men. Even then, as today, homes were filled with growing plants and flowers in an effort to add a little beauty and decoration to the drabness. Outside the kitchen window a tree was invariably planted. Kept alive by left over dishwater, it served to shade the window and give a more cheerful and filtered view of the desert from within

Continued on Page 67

A reign of terror
is launched by
Col. William Thompson:

Central Oregon Dictator

by David Braly

Col. William Thompson
(Courtesy of Crook Couny Historical Society)

When we hear of people who fear their own local officials, of hit squads serving a dictator colonel, of a landowning oligarchy keeping small farmers and townsfolk under thumb by the use of organized terror, we think of Central America.

But in March, 1882, such a dictatorship under Col. William Thompson emerged in Central Oregon. Thompson's control of the region began after an incident involving Lucius Langdon, owner of a small ranch near Willow Creek under Grizzly Mountain. On March 15, 1882, Langdon found 2 axes and a partially cut tree behind his fence, but on property claimed by A.H. Crooks, a follower of Col. William Thompson, leader of a group of big ranchers who wanted to control the region. Langdon suspected that the axes belonged to Crooks and Crooks' son-in-law Stephen J. Jory.

He was right.

Crooks and Jory had been called home for lunch at noon by their wives. Langdon was waiting for them

when they returned. He shot both men dead.

Langdon mounted his horse and headed for his brother George's Mill Creek ranch. He wanted money to go to the county seat 125 miles north in The Dalles, where he intended to surrender to the authorities.

Garrett Maupin had heard the shots while riding near Langdon's ranch and he rode over to investigate, arriving just in time to see Langdon leaving. Maupin found the two dead men lying in the snow on a knoll behind Langdon's barn. He hurried to Prineville, the only town in central Oregon at that time, to report the murders. Soon men from Prineville arrived at the Langdon ranch to view the dead men.

Two posses were formed. Col. Thompson led one to George Langdon's cabin, but a barking dog alerted Lucius of their approach. He fled across the snow on foot. Tracking him was impossible as night fell.

Another posse proceeded to Lucius Langdon's ranch in hopes their quarry had doubled back. He had.

Once again a barking dog alerted Langdon. He fled, and had already leaped into a saddle and galloped off when the posse's leader got close enough to yell at him. When Langdon realized that James Blakely led this posse and not Thompson, he reined in and surrendered. The posse had dinner with the Langdons and their children before they took Lucius into Prineville.

Blakely turned Langdon over to Deputy Sheriff John Luckey. Luckey had local blacksmith W.C. Foren put irons on Langdon. Foren was also the deputy marshal and joined Luckey guarding Langdon at the Jackson House hotel. They planned to take him to The Dalles in the morning.

Luckey and Foren also arrested W.C. Harrison. Blakely had been given a warrant for Harrison's arrest but had refused to serve it because he knew that Harrison was in town when Crooks and Jory were murdered. In fact, Harrison had joined James and his brother Joe Blakely when they rode out to view the bodies with other men from town. Harrison, an employee of Langdon's had been at Langdon's ranch when Blakely arrived and had decided to accompany them to town.

About 3 a.m. the hotel door was suddenly thrown open. A dozen masked men with drawn pistols rushed in, overpowered the deputies, and shot Langdon to death on the sofa where he lay.

One version of what happened next says that the masked men tied and blindfolded the deputies, then grabbed Harrison for having said that what happened to Crooks and Jory "served them right."

A more likely version (considering the sources) is that the killers were milling around the hotel with Harrison and others for a long time after Langdon's death, unmasked. When Harrison said of Langdon, "Well, he was always good to me," they grabbed him. Harrison pleaded for his life as they dragged him out of the hotel. "I've got a little boy," he cried.

There is full agreement about what happened next. While frightened townsfolk listened inside their darkened houses to Harrison begging fo his life and for someone to save him, a rope was placed around his neck. A masked man jumped onto a horse, took the other end of the rope, and galloped down the street dragging Harrison behind him. Harrison's body was later hung from the iron bridge that spanned Crooked River on the west edge of town.

A crowd watched at dawn as Harrison's body was carried back into town to the accompaniment of the wild ringing of the school bell. The crowd then went to view the bridge.

These murders launched Vigilante rule in central Oregon. The Vigilantes, or "vigilanters" as they were sometimes called, were led by Col. William Thompson.

Thompson later claimed in his fanciful autobiography that he had been inside the hotel when the Vigilantes broke in and that they had held *him* at gunpoint!

Thompson was about thirty-five years old in 1882. He witnessed his first lynching when he was five, crossing the plains in a wagon train. He later said that the hanging of "the trembling, writhing, begging wretch" was "burned into my brain with letters of fire, never to be effaced while memory holds her sway."

Raised near Eugene, the son of a harsh schoolmaster, Thompson joined the eastern Oregon gold rush when he was fourteen. He afterwards worked for poet Joachim Miller, first for his Idaho pony express company and then for his newspapers in Eugene. The federal government

suppressed the newspapers several times for printing anti-administration articles. Thompson himself later became an owner of newspapers, first in Eugene and then in Salem. Once he shot to death two brothers who were competing with him. His first kill, however, had been an Indian he shot in the back.

By the time Thompson and his brother George bought six ranches in the Hay and Little Creek areas of Wasco County, he had great influence at Salem. George had been a state

But people were not fleeing central Oregon to escape because they were "hard characters" who feared quick justice, as Thompson claimed. They were escaping Thompson's dictatorship and its accompanying reign of terror.

senator and another brother was a Lane County judge. Thompson himself had become famous in the state as a spokesman for the Salem leadership and as the "mad-cap Colonel" who behaved so recklessly during the Modoc War.

When he acquired the ranches, Thompson moved into a Prineville house at the southwest corner of West Fourth and Claypool streets. His across-the-street neighbor was a thirty-year-old man who was more respected than Thompson but who lacked his powerful connections: James Blakely.

Thompson ran central Oregon after the murders of March 1882. The modern counties of Crook, Deschutes and Jefferson were his, but possibly his power also embraced modern Lake, Grant, Wheeler, Harney and Wasco counties. Allied to Thompson

throughout this vast area — a third of the state — were the big ranchers and their hired men. *Oregonian* editor Harvey Scott claimed that if Thompson wanted any man in three counties dead the man was as good as buried.

Few people dared to criticize Thompson. To do so was to speak against a ruthless, powerful man, but perhaps just as important, to oppose the economic and political masters of the entire region. People who did talk unfavorably of him or his gunmen received a skull-and-crossbones note, a warning from the Vigilantes to "cheese it" or face death. The Blakely brothers, John Combs, Steve Staats, Sam Smith, Al Schwartz and a handful of other men refused to knuckle under, but two thousand people in central Oregon were terrorized into silence.

In October 1882, when Crook County (the modern counties of Crook, Deschutes, Jefferson and southwest Wheeler) was carved out of Wasco, Col. Thompson's influence in Salem paid off for the Vigilantes. Gov. Moody appointed Thompson's brother county judge and appointed other gang members to county offices.

The same week the four men were murdered, Thompson and his allies had formed the Ochoco Livestock Association. This Vigilante organization soon announced that no one could ride across Crook County rangeland without its written permission. Most men complied. A few refused. James Blakely, who owned a ranch near Grizzly Mountain, purchased six revolvers and distributed them to his riders to use if Vigilantes bothered them.

Al Schwartz was another man who defied the Vigilantes, Schwartz had a family and a small ranch near Prineville. During the night of Dec. 24, 1882, Schwartz entered Burmeister's saloon, where Vigilantes persuaded him to join their card game. He did, but took care to sit facing the door. Unfortunately, although he kept his back to the wall, the wall had a window in it. A Vigilante outside shot Schwartz twice in the head through the closed window, killing him instantly.

The night of murder had only begun.

Vigilantes were angry about losing money they'd bet on a horse race. The race's winner, a youth named Charles Luster, was staying at Schwartz's ranch. Luster had been asked to throw the race but hadn't. Now the Vigilantes lured him and his friend Sidney Huston to W.C. Barnes' house. There, they attacked them. Huston was armed. He shot and fatally wounded W.C. Foren, the same deputy marshal who had been "guarding" Langdon and Harrison the night they were murdered. But the boys were overpowered. They were both hanged from a juniper tree, then shot through the backs of their heads. James Blakely and Sam Smith found their bodies Christmas morning.

Skull-and-crossbones notices were posted around Prineville immediately after these latest murders. Thompson claimed later that these notices drove rustlers and their allies out of the region. "There was then such a higera as has seldom been witnessed," he wrote. "Men not before suspicioned skipped the country. They stood not upon the order of their going, but went — and went in a hurry. Among the number was an ex-Justice of the Peace."

But people were not fleeing central Oregon to escape because they were "hard characters" who feared quick justice, as Thompson claimed. They were escaping Thompson's dictatorship and its accompanying reign of terror.

The murders continued. Like those of the "Red Christmas," they went unpunished. Vigilantes blew of the head of Steve Staats at Stearns Butte. Shorty Davis, a Prineville area rancher, was the first of two men with that name to simply vanish after cattlemen became annoyed by his existence.

James Blakely and Hank Vaughn were harder to kill.

One Sunday night Blakely's defiance was discussed by Vigilantes meeting in a Prineville saloon. County Treasurer Gus Winckler was unwisely overhead to say that Blakely would have to be taken up the hill to the cemetery "feet first." These words were reported to Blakely almost immediately. The Vigilantes had already left when Blakely, John Combs, Sam Smith and the Wagner brothers burst into the saloon looking for them. The next morning Blakely found Winckler hiding from him in an outdoor toilet behind the Jackson House. Blakely ordered him out of the privy, then told him to leave town on the next stagecoach or else he wouldn't leave Prineville ever. Winckler left, never to return.

Thompson allegedly put gunfighter Charlie Long up to confronting Hank Vaughn. Long had ridden with Thompson during the Bannock War; Vaughn, also a gunfighter, was a close friend of Blakely's. They faced each other inside the saloon of Til Glaze, himself a gunfighter who had

James Blakely
(Courtesy of Crook County Historical Society)

Blakely led 80 mounted Moonshiners into Prineville, all of them unmasked. They rode calmly but fully armed down the main street of the dusty little cow town.

ridden in Thompson's posse during the hunt for Langdon but who was a friend of Blakely. Long shot Vaughn through the left breast and creased his scalp, while Vaughn shot Long three times in his left shoulder. Both men survived.

Another shooting was cut and dried. Mossy Barnes was playing cards in Dick Graham's saloon with Mike Mogan in the spring of 1883. Barnes claimed that Mogan owed him six dollars and demanded immediate payment. When Mogan could not pay, Barnes drew a pistol. "Why, Mossy, you wouldn't shoot me," said Mogan quietly. Barnes' answer was to shoot him through his lungs. Mogan managed to stagger out of the saloon, then across the street to a livery stable where he had left his

own gun. He started back with it, but collapsed in the street. Before dying a few days later, Mogan told his brother Frank and other visitors that he had recognized the gun used by Barnes as one belonging to his former employer, Col. William Thompson.

Frank Mogan said publicly that Barnes had used Thompson's gun. The Colonel decided Frank Mogan was talking too much. Mogan was standing at the bar in Kelley's saloon on Dec. 18, 1883, his back to the door, and failed to see Thompson enter. The Colonel crept up behind him, put his pistol to the back of Mogan's neck, and pulled the trigger. Thompson later bragged that Mogan "fell with more than one bullet through his body" and this time he spoke the truth. Thompson emptied his pistol into the dead man.

Thompson sent for Sheriff George Churchill and surrendered himself. Churchill told him to go home. Thompson then asked the committing magistrate to place him under bonds to appear before the grand jury. This was just for show. The Vigilante-controlled grand jury returned a verdict of "not a true bill."

The girl who had married Mike Mogan and then married his brother Frank sued this man who had twice widowed her. She was awarded $3600. Thompson never paid it.

But the murders of the Mogans outraged the community. People were finally willing to risk giving their support to men who opposed Thompson.

Organized opposition began with a secret meeting called one night during the winter of 1883-84 by Rev. T. Clay Neese at the Stewart & Pett flour mill near Prineville. There Neese, Pett, David Stewart, James Blakely, John Combs and Sam Smith organized the Citizens Protective Union to combat the Vigilantes. The Vigilantes dubbed them "the moonshiners" because they met at night by the light of the moon. The name stuck and was borne proudly by members of the organization.

Patrolling the countryside and communicating by cipher, the Moonshiners grew and quickly gained public support. Al Lyle and David Templeton of Prineville led a bipartisan political effort by the Moonshiners to seize control o the county government when the first election was held June 2, 1884.

When lawyer George Barnes (Mossy's brother) declared that the Vigilantes would destroy the Moonshiners, the latter decided that it was time for a showdown. Blakely led eighty mounted Moonshiners into

Prineville, all of them unmasked. They rode calmly but fully armed down the main street of the dusty little cow town. Vigilantes fled into Til Glaze's saloon, where they peered at Blakely through the windows. The Moonshiners formed a semi-circle in front, then Blakely challenged the Vigilantes to come outside and fight. The Vigilantes stayed where they were.

Public fear became public contempt. The Vigilantes' hold on central Oregon was shattered.

Thompson decided to git while the gitting was good. The Thompsons sold their ranches to Amos Dunham, then slept in Dunham's barn beside their guns until they left for California.

The Moonshiners won the county election. The new sheriff, Blakely, ran out the Vigilante gunmen, but could not touch the powerful families who led the gang. Although a nonviolent struggle between the Vigilantes and the Moonshiners continued for many years, peace and liberty returned to central Oregon until the turn of the century. At that time, the Vigilantes briefly and viciously resumed their depredations as the Crook County Sheep Shooting Association. But that's another story.

Later day office-holding Vigilantes saw to it that Crook County records touching upon their atrocities disappeared. One historian commented upon the vanishing records as early as 1905. Some prominent Crook County families claim to have arrived in the area later than they did. Others say that their ancestors were Moonshiners when in fact they were Vigilantes.

Charlie Long was shot to death in Washington. Hank Vaughn was killed when his horse fell upon him when he rode it onto a Pendleton sidewalk. Til Glaze was slain with another man during a gunfight in Burns. Mossy Barnes committed suicide. George Barnes was shot to death in Canyon City. James Blakely, who later became a sheriff and prominent rancher in Umatilla County, was grand marshal of Prineville's Crooked River Roundup shortly before his death in 1953 at the age of 101.

And the dictator himself?

Thompson occasionally returned to Prineville to visit friends, but he edited a newspaper in Alturas, California until his death.

Once Thompson warned in his newspaper that unless outlawry around Alturas ended, mob action might occur. Shortly afterward, five men were lynched — from a bridge.

Although a nonviolent struggle between the Vigilantes and the Moonshiners continued for many years, peace and liberty returned to central Oregon until the turn of the century.

DUST, JACKS & MATRIMONY VINES
Continued from Page 63

Continued from Page 63

the house. These trees were called "matrimony" vines and some are still growing today against the sides of abandoned homesteader's cabins.

In 1911, Doc selected the best area for William's and Leon's well and digging commenced. Doc's well was only fifteen feet deep and it was thought this new well would not exceed this dimension. However, the depth of water tables on the desert was very deceiving, even for Doc, and after many days of arduous digging and reaching twenty feet with no sign of any moisture, discouragement set in, even though Doc assured them that the deeper they went the better the water they would find. He admitted that his own water was much too alkali for drinking and washing. Someone, not Doc, who threw up his arms in dispair at such an idea, suggested using dynamite; and, although no one knew exactly how to go about planting the explosive in the well shaft, the dynamite was procured, put into place and ignited. The resulting explosion was heard for miles, and its impact sent Leon, William, Doc and several curious spectators sprawling, but it served its purpose and the now forty foot hole it generated bubbled with the best tasting, softest water around. It was indeed an achievement and Ada's champagne, which arrived several weeks later, was enjoyed by the many homesteaders who came for the well's christening.

Today, one can find no traces of the well, nor of Leon's, William's or Doc's cabins, nor even of the town of Cliff. Nature has carefully obliterated any trace of man. There is still talk of irrigating the desert and transforming it into productive farm land but so far little has been done. William's and Leon's one square mile is still owned by their descendents and in one corner is a rather new shanty owned by one of Arthur's grandchildren, a merchant seaman who lives there during several months of the year. For him, the homestead land seems just as exciting now as it did for his great grandfather and grand uncle seventy years before. For him and others like him, it is still virgin area where a person can escape the artificial complexities of modern day living, compete with the adversities of nature and enjoy the great pleasures of a real, undisturbed and uncluttered world.

Editor's Note: The author is a grandson of William and a nephew of Leon.

BUTTE COUNTRY

butte byut *n:* an emminence rising abruptly from flat land surrounding it.

Black Butte (6.436') as seen from the Camp Sherman area. (Geoff Hill Photo)

By Russ Baehr

When the youthful Cascade volcanoes had stopped making their brags, scores of buttes had raised their collective heads.

Webster called them: "An emminence rising abruptly from flat land surrounding it." Central Oregon's array of these miniature mountains, or overgrown hills, outnumber their kind in most of the other western states.

Each dormant elevation is a huge cinder heap that is a joy to the state's highway departments. They supply a seemingly unlimited supply of cinders for road beds, and for grits for combating our five months of winter.

Their names are as colorful, varied and contrasting as the buttes themselves. For starters, how about Four Mile, Five Mile and Six Mile buttes, lying west and somewhat north of the town of Sisters? Four miles from what? Six miles from where? It is a mystery that died with the passing of the oldtime Oregon loggers and early foresters.

Numerically speaking, they have a cousin, Sixteen Butte some thirty-five miles southeast of Bend, and a small fry relative, Quarter Butte at desert's edge near Jayne's Well.

In the naming process, the animals have all left their prints in the lineup. Coyote, Cat, Ground Hog, Antelope, Buck, Mutton, Marmot, Deer, Studhorse and Bear Wallow. Someone saw to it that the four-footed creatures were all well represented.

Mrs. Stella Nelson of Bend had a son born while she and her husband were living in the Cat Butte logging camp about nine miles southeast of

Bend. But she said that butte was later renamed Bessie, and Bessie Butte it remains today. Perhaps changed to the name of one of the log bosses' wives?

The names are colorful. Green, Gray, Burnt, Firestone, Black, Cinnamon and Blackrock certainly add color to the butte language.

All of the early Deschutes National Forest maps of the '30's, '40's and '50's listed Bachelor Butte as that — a butte. But the ski buffs soon took steps which they felt would add prestige to the newly developed ski area. So a name change was submitted to the proper authorities to make that landmark a mountain. The authorities concurred, and man made a mountain out of a butte.

Some of these land masses give their occupational lineage also. Ranger, Pilot, Teller, Abbot, Trappers and Hunter. Others retained a kind of family status, as in Orphan, Bachelor, Husband, Wife and Company.

Wigtop Butte, at the south perimeter of the forest hard by Devil's Garden, doubtless got that moniker from the look of growth around its crest. Many of these desert elevations have clusters of mountain mahogany or stunted junipers on their upper slopes. Others are capped with snowbrush or manzanita, two leafy shrubs that hold their tough green leaves all winter.

As we move west into the pine belt, there are fine stands of Ponderosas colonnading their slopes. Nearer the Cascade Range, fir, hemlock, spruce, Jackpine and sugarpine intermix with the cinnamon-barked Ponderosa.

Foresters, loggers, and discerning hunters and hikers will note that certain evergreens grow at specified altitudes. A hunter-logger companion of earlier years, told me how one could judge how high he was by the presence of certain trees on the ridges and buttes, such as white fir or hemlock at about 4000 to 5000 feet.

From the thirties to the fifties, numerous buttes were hosts for lonely forest fire lookouts manning their towers. C.E. 'Slim' Hein, a long time forestry man in the Deschutes area, is a walking encyclopedia of much trivia. It was with great good fortune I could pick his memory for much of the following.

Slim helped build the Spring Butte tower in 1931, and was the first to man it. He told of the crow's nest at the Summit Stage Butte where the fireman had to shinny up a pine to scan the surrounding forest expanse. Other rare bits told of a lookout on Fort Rock's west point, topside—and of the town of Sisters' lookout in the top of a huge snag, with its crow's nest. Others, Bates' Butte (after an early day family) and Plot Butte had only a tent and fire finder for their primitive equipment, and were only used for a year or two. In the Deschutes National Forest area, he could recall 42 buttes having towers.

For some buttes—for many—the only time of the year that man will ever set foot on them will be during Oregon's deer season. Yet, they are a constant source of unique finds for one that slows his pace and climbs a few each year.

A SAMPLER OF CENTRAL OREGON BUTTE NAMES

Four Mile	Marmot	Bachelor	Kwinnum	Cabin
Five Mile	Bear Wallow	Husband	Pilpil	Wing
Six Mile	Bessie	Wigtop	Ipsoot	Saddle
Coyote	Ranger	Frederick	Salt	Dugout
Cat	Pilot	Hampton	Dry	China Hat
Ground Hog	Abbot	Glass	Box	No Name
Mutton	Orphan	Lumrum	Benchmark	

BELOW: Lava Butte (5.016′) located 10 miles south of Bend. Photo courtesy Oregon State Highway Travel Division.

The butte names are a constant source of amusement — or amazement. They roll off the tongue like syrup. Lumrum, Kwinnum, Pilpil, Kweo, Topso, Lowullo, Ipsoot.

Twisted clinkers that oozed out of hot crevasses are sometimes one to two feet long, spiralled or curved like giant bananas. Lava bombs are another curiosity that are formed in the eruptions. They run from peanut size to fifty gallon oil drum mass. Most are oval shaped, having a raised eye on one side.

Persevere to the tops of these lonely outposts and one will find a richness of silvered, weathered wood, unbelievable in its charm. Wood sentinals that long ago lost the battle with the elements on these harsh crests, moan and creak in the incessant winds, winds that scour and etch a loveliness seldom seen in any other condition. These weathered wonders make an elegant piece for a rugged rock garden, or atop a $500.00 coffee table.

Many of these conical hills bear faint evidences of trappers working the areas, years earlier. Trees notched three to four feet off the ground held trap sets for certain animals. A sapling was laid against the cut to make a convenient runway or ramp, from the ground to the bait. By now, these cuts have been softened and rounded with almost a century's growth of bark on their edges.

Central Oregon is overrun with these landmarks and they continue east and south towards Wagontire Mt. In particular, three come to mind: Frederick, Hampton, and Glass Buttes. Each differs in composition, size and contour from the other. Turn south off the Bend-Burns highway at the fifty mile post and Frederick will be the main landmark on the drive through a desolate expanse on the route to the Lost Forest and the sand dunes. It is a jumble of lava and basalt.

The larger Hampton Butte is the halfway post between the run from Bend to Burns. It is rich in various agates, geodes and petrified woods. Pioneer settlers told of two gold finds there.

Glass Butte lies south of that highway at the 75 mile post. This venerable landmass was the ammunition dump for many Indian tribes because of the unlimited supply of glassy obsidian it provided. Tools, scrapers, finger knives, eared points and spear heads were roughly fashioned there, then later finished to perfection when needed.

How far reaching the Indian trade moved out of this sector was proven by the find of a Glass Butte point in a Maryland dig. Two others turned up in Ohio. Yes, archaeologists and geologists can fingerprint the various obsidians, some forty in all.

The butte names are a constant source of amusement—or amazement. They roll off the tongue like syrup. Lumrum, Kwinnum, Pilpil, Kweo, Topso, Lowullo, Ipsoot.

What are their origins? Certainly the rough cut and hard working lumberjacks did not dream such a linguistic largess. According to Slim Heim, the man responsible for the Indian designations' being used was Walt Perry, an old forester who served in the Bend-Sisters area from 1915 to 1925.

Many such are listed in McArthur's Oregon names as a result of his concern for their spelling and continued use, and a carrying on of the heritage of Oregon's tribes.

With such a galaxy of outcroppings, it was inevitable that the names would run from the poetic to the prosaic. Salt, Dry, Sand, Lavatop, Pumice, Box, Corral, Benchmark, Cabin, Wing, Saddle, Dugout and China Hat are descriptive of some of the unique features.

For some reason, the letter 'K' stands out in the titles of many. No less than eighteen, from Ko to Ketchketch are sprinkled throughout this inland sector.

In passing years, this writer has camped at the desert's edge countless times and surveyed the singular profiles of certain buttes, as dawn hid them layered in fog, or revealed them as a cold morning sun glinted off a rim or pine sentinal, identifying each.

Dozens more I have climbed slowly, walking in trails not made by man. From a fine vantage point, I have eaten my sandwich as I warmed in a pale October sun or chilled, huddled in a sheltered refuge against a sudden fall storm.

Many I will never climb, nor will thousands of other Oregonians. They extend, seemingly, endlessly through the abyss of desert space, southeast past the Great Basin.

There are too many. They are too remote, too removed from roads and byways. These phantom hills number about 180 in the environs of the Deschutes National Forest alone.

So they will remain, legendary places of poetic names, dreamed of on a hunt or hike that will never be..., Ooskan, Kweo, Polytop.

In the naming, the long and short of it, the butte namers finally ran out. Near the margin of the low desert hard by Devils' Garden, lies the last: No Name Butte.

Oregonians might well start a 'Butte of the Month Club.' Its climbing members might, with good luck, complete their task in twenty-some years. ∎

Narcissa Whitman, drawn by Olive W. Dixon after her death. (Photo courtesy Oregon Historical Society).

Missionary MOM

Narcissa Prentiss Whitman was one of the first two white women to cross the Rockies...

By Joanne McCubrey

Vivacious, blond Narcissa Prentiss Whitman, missionary to the Northwest Indians in the mid 1800's and foster mother to 11 children, was a good humored, dynamic and impulsive woman with a strong sense of adventure. Her grey eyes and high spirited beauty charmed rough mountain men as well as her doctor-missionary husband.

Narcissa was one of the first two white women to cross the Rockies and, in doing so, blazed a trail for thousands to follow. In the end, her massacre at the hands of the Indians she sought to help caused such a public uproar that the Oregon territory was created.

Narcissa was born, the third of nine children of Stephen and Clarissa Ward Prentiss of Prattsburg, New York on March 14, 1808. She was a dutiful child and the favorite of her parents.

She attended the Franklin Academy (a Presbyterian sponsored secondary school) where she was courted by shy, awkward Henry Spalding. He hoped for marriage but she rejected his proposal and began teaching school in Prattsburg.

In the fall of 1834, the Reverend

Samuel Parker, who wanted to bring Christianity to the Indians in the West, came to New York seeking both donations and recruits for his mission. Narcissa heard Parker speak and offered her services, but the board would not accept a single woman.

Parker had, however, enlisted Dr. Marcus Whitman, who had been courting Narcissa. Whitman proposed to Narcissa and was accepted. Soon afterward he left with Parker on a fact-finding trip west and was gone for nearly a year. He got as far as the fur trading rendezvous at Green River, Wyoming and confirmed what he wanted to know. If wagons could travel over the Rockies, then women could cross the rugged mountains as well.

Marcus returned east and, in February of 1835, married Narcissa, who wore a homemade puritan black bombazine dress. Shortly after the wedding they set off on their long trip west.

Whitman picked Henry Spalding and his new wife Eliza to travel to Oregon with the Whitmans ... the same Henry Spalding who had been rejected by Narcissa several years earlier. Spalding, even though now married, remained bitter and was spitefully jealous of Marcus.

The party experienced several delays in the beginning. This was the first time women had attempted the overland journey to Oregon, and there was a reluctance to escort them; but they joined a caravan of the American Fur Company and started west with a sense of adventure and discovery.

Weeks later, the wagons clattered into the Green River rendezvous, disembarking in the midst of hundreds of Indians, trappers and mountain men. Narcissa and Eliza were immediate curiosities, impressing such renowned mountain men as Joseph Meek and Jim Bridger. Marcus had earned Bridger's respect on his earlier trip by removing an arrowhead which had been embedded in the mountain man's back. When the doctor mentioned the lack of infection, Bridger is said to have remarked, "meat don't spoil in the Rockies."

After leaving Green River, the trip became more tedious. The party's wagons dwindled to a two-wheel cart, however Narcissa remained cheerful. Her health was good and she enjoyed the buffalo meat they had to eat when food became less plentiful. They finally reached Fort Walla Walla after nearly seven months of travel.

The Whitmans established their mission among the Cayuse Indians

Whitman/Spalding Monument. (Photo courtesy Oregon Historical Society).

Narcissa's sense of adventure, individualism, and Christian zeal carried her into territory where no woman had ventured before.

Sketch of the Whitman Mission by H. D. Nichols. (Photo courtesy Oregon Historical Society).

at Waiilatpu, in spite of warnings to the contrary. The Spaldings went 125 miles away to work with the Nez Perce in what is now western Idaho.

Narcissa taught in the mission school while Marcus conducted services, practiced medicine, and taught the Indians the basics of farming.

Narcissa's only child, Alice Clarissa, was born on Narcissa's own birthday, March 14, 1837. The child charmed the entire mission but was tragically drowned in the Walla Walla River when she was only 2 years old. This catapulted Narcissa into a severe depression. She began to take in foster children, including seven children from a single family whose parents had died on the trail. She was also a foster mother to the daughters of both Joe Meek and Jim Bridger as well as several others.

Narcissa was a good mother to her 11 adopted children, firm but good humored. The children she mothered must have helped relieve her depression in the years following the untimely death of her beloved Alice Clarissa, and may have eased the constant exhaustion and solitude of her lonely home, for it was a difficult life in Oregon. The language and cultural barriers were tremendous and the Indians were not as desirous of being converted as the Whitmans had originally been told. The situation was not helped by the internal discord among the missionaries, created mainly by Spalding's bitterness and jealousy of Whitman.

The mission became a stopping place for immigrants who arrived, exhausted and hungry, to rest for the last lap of their journey. More and more travelers were coming west, and by the middle 1840's, the Indians were becoming nervous with the influx of whites coming to their land. They began to blame the Whitmans for being the forerunners of the migrations to Oregon. In 1847, in the midst of this mistrust, the western immigrants brought a measles epidemic to the mission.

The settlers' children, with their natural immunity, responded well to Marcus' treatments, but the Indian children died in large numbers. The Indians brooded and fumed, feeling that their children had died due to the Whitmans. By late November, they could no longer hold back their anger. On a cold and wet November 29, 1847, a small band of Cayuse warriors with guns and tomahawks descended on Waiilatpu and murdered Narcissa, as well as Marcus and 12 other settlers. Narcissa was 39 years old.

The tragic news was carried east by Joe Meek. Narcissa's long time admirer and whose cousin was married to President Polk. He so aroused and influenced public opinion that only nine months after the massacre, Congress created the Oregon territory and Joe Meek was appointed U.S. Marshall. Five Cayuse warriors were tried and hung.

Narcissa's sense of adventure, indivudalism, and Christian zeal carried her into territory where no woman had ventured before. She rebounded from tragedy with an outpouring of love for the many homeless children she took into her home. Narcissa paved the way for countless others to follow the trail she had blazed with such hope and enthusiasm. ■

Oregon's Deluge

*Without warning,
one of the nation's most overlooked
disasters occurred in tiny Heppner, Oregon . . .*

Within hours, tiny Willow Creek had returned to its banks (TOP) after sweeping through Heppner (BOTTOM) leaving death and destruction in its wake.   Photo courtesy Oregon Historical Society.

By Francis X. Sculley

Everyone has heard of the bursting of the South Fork Dam above Johnston, Pennsylvania on May 31, 1889. In disasters involving the release of pent-up water, that debacle ranks first throughout the world. Out of a population of thirty thousand in the path of the destroyer, twenty-two hundred were swept to their death. Nonetheless, there is a small community in Oregon that suffered proportionately as great a loss. What is more Heppner, Oregon had not a second's warning, whereas it was known for days that Johnston was in peril. Neither did the Oregon disaster involve weeks of prolonged rain. Had it not been for two heroic range riders who carried the warning to the valley below, the casualty list might have been as great as Johnstown. Yet how many Americans have ever read of Heppner?

Tiny Willow Creek, which bisects the Oregon community, flows from south to north and is barely six feet wide during a normal summer. It is so shallow that kids can play in perfect safety. Yet on Sunday, June 14, 1903, during the midst of supper hour the tiny creek was transformed into a raging Niagara, an avalanche of water that swept 247 people to eternity and threatened 3,000 others. Buildings were crushed into matchwood and swept down the valley. Within an hour after the first awful rush, Willow Creek was a gentle kitten in a desolate valley. Destruction was enormous.

Heppner had anticipated rain for several days, as the fall had been much lighter than usual. The hillsides and fields were as brown as leather, and clouds of choking dust enveloped everything. Morrow County could "stand a good soaking" if the crops were going to amount to anything.

On Friday, June 12, two aged Indian women appeared at the warehouse of the Morrow County Land and Trust Company to sell a small amount of carded wool. As it looked like rain — and perhaps due to other commitments, R. F. Hynd, Manager of the facility was a bit brusque. He urged the women to conclude their business and hurry off, lest they be caught in a downpour.

"You look out. Not long great water come — Take Boston man, papoose, horse, houses and everything to Columbia," warned one of the annoyed women.

Few who heard the comment were anything but amused. The dire prediction came back to haunt survivors in the days that followed. To this day, the story is often told in Heppner and it has become part of the folklore of the community.

Sunday was a warm, sticky day, and there was a threat of rain throughout the early afternoon hours. By three o'clock the sky to the south of the little city (1,000 constitutes a city in Oregon) was as dark as ink, rent from time to time by livid flashes of lightning. The continuous rumble of thunder sounded like the approach of a tornado.

"Somewhere they are getting a heavy shower — Heaven knows we need it," was the general comment, though some commented they had never seen a sky so ominous.

To the south, the skies opened over the mountains sending cascading torrents down upon the slopes in almost unbelievable volume. It is estimated that three inches of rain fell in less than an hour. A vertical wall of water slammed into the narrow gorge with such force as to

flatten small trees. Millions of gallons of water plus huge boulders, poured into a narrow trough, which could not possibly hold the fall. Willow Creek above Heppner was converted into a raging avalanche of dirty brown water interlaced with boulders, trees and everything in its path. Compressed into a narrow canyon, it was vainly trying to liberate itself. Sweeping everything before it, and growing in size every minute, the destroyer moved northward toward Heppner, which was blissfully unaware of the approach of doom.

Shortly before five o'clock, Willow Creek was a monstrous lake on the move, flexing its muscles for a go at the little towns in its path. Preceded by a few thunderclaps and flashes of lightning, the huge wall of water bore down on Heppner. No one was aware of their peril until water began to pour down Main Street.

The water did not rush over the top of Heppner, as in the case of Johnstown or the earlier flood in Williamsburg, Massachusetts (May 16, 1874). People were unaware of anything out of the ordinary until a brown river rushed through the city. At the south end of Heppner, the flood had created a solid dam out of debris. This, coupled with the rubble in the channel, kept the height of the water at housetop level. Heppner had many homes that rested flat upon the ground, or at best were simple stone foundations. These were wrested from the ground, tossed high in the air, landing on others, creating an enormous pile up. This, in turn would impede the progress of the water, thus creating another dam. This would

TOP: Piles of debris remained after the flood waters had receded. BOTTOM: The Ayer House was carried six blocks by the wall of water. Photos courtesy Oregon Historical Society.

burst creating new devastation. The water never had a chance to spread out across the valley where its force could have been nullified.

Boiling from their homes like ants from a hill, the town's citizens made a frenzied rush for the hills that bordered the community. Those who lived on the east side had a short run to safety. With the screaming of women and children, and the terrified whinnying of horses, added to the roar and the crushing of buildings upon one another, Heppner was about to cross the river Styx. But many of them made it. Those who headed for the hills on the westside had to run directly in front of the flood. Few of them made it, but there

The flood ripped through the heart of Heppner's residential district.   Photo courtesy Oregon Historical Society.

was no time to count heads now.

From the heights above, those who made it watched in mute horror the destruction of the town. Like an arrow through a giant cheese, the flood ripped through the very heart of the residential district. Poplars two feet in diameter were snapped off like cornstalks.

Dan Salter, who had lost his wife and six of his children, escaped with one of his kiddies by climbing into an old dry goods box. With this crude craft, he shot the rapids, though more by accident than design. He was washed ashore, more dead than alive. He had seen dozens of heads disappear beneath the waves during his miraculous ride.

At the moment the water slammed into Heppner, Leslie Matlock and Bruce Kelly, two experienced range riders appeared on the scene.

"My God! Lexington and Ione (to the north). There are hundreds in the path of this water. Can we beat the flood?" shouted Matlock as he pointed at the water with his wirecutter. History recalls the ride of Paul Revere, Israel Bissel, and Caesar Rodney, but somehow manages to overlook the Oregon pair. Digging in their spurs and applying their whips vigorously the pair launched their life saving ride. Straight uphill at times, then through fields with five and six foot barbed wire fences every few hundred yards, they raced toward Lexington. Twice Matlock's horse fell, the last time pinning its rider's leg beneath, but Matlock got back in the saddle, even though he was lacerated in a dozen places from the cruel barbed wire. The

gallant equine had made a little history as it dropped dead in the center of Lexington. Over 1,000 lives had been saved.

As the people ran for the safety of the hills, fresh horses were procured and the gallant riders headed toward Ione. Not one life had been lost. Had they been fifteen minutes later, Lexington would have suffered the fate of Heppner.

Due to the degree of drop, the riders easily outdistanced the flood to Ione. The townsfolk were about to start church services when Matlock and Kelly burst upon the scene. Few believed the pair, and some suggested they had been drinking. It was not long before they knew differently as a wall of water and debris bore down on the community. All made it safely to the hills. By the time the villagers had a chance to apologize to the badly spent pair — they were gone. They had saved over 2,000 lives by their heroic, grueling ride.

So they departed into the pages of Oregon history and folklore.

Within the hour the flood waters had receded, and before the coming of darkness, the task of searching for the bodies had begun. The waiting room of the First National Bank and Robert's Hall were converted into a temporary morgue, and as one body after another was brought into the receiving center, the grim task of identification began. The very heartbeat of the town had almost ceased to be; an entire generation of small children had perished in the flood — one of history's most unusual.

The residential district, one of the most beautiful in Morrow County,

was scrubbed bare, with a mountainous pile of debris pushed to the outer fringes of the path of the waters. The channel was but a block and a half wide and within this area there were few survivors.

With the coming of daylight on Monday the fifteenth, the entire surviving community was afoot, searching through the ruins for the bodies of friends and neighbors. It was a heart rending task. From throughout Oregon came offers of help, gifts of cash and volunteer aid. Condolences from throughout the United States poured into the office of Major Frank Gilliam. Several towns in the State which had planned celebrations during the summer, announced that all proceeds would go to the flood-ravaged city. The people of the State were magnificent.

As the long casualty list was posted, a total of 247 dead was recorded. However, it is a certainty that several more transients perished in the disaster. According to historians several more bodies were recovered from the Columbia River several weeks later. Perhaps a true list of casualties will never be known.

There was no warning. The rainfall was not general and people a few miles away were appalled at the enormity of the disaster.

It was one of the nation's most overlooked disasters, and perhaps its most overlooked. Another thing: Matlock and Kelly were both teetotalers all the way, few would have blamed them had they both embibed after what they had seen and endured. Lexington and Ione never forgot the heroics of the pair.

FOURTH OF JULY–
Central Oregon Style

By Donna Meddish

Fourth of July, 1916. Corner of Wall Street and Oregon Avenue. Photo by Claude Kelley.

BOOM! The city of Bend was awakened at sunrise on the Fourth of July of 1921 by a monstrous charge of dynamite from Awbrey Heights. It was followed by smaller successive blasts sounding out our year of Independence, 1-7-7-6. Moments later, a second series of dynamite blasts, this time from atop Pilot Butte, boomed out 1-9-2-1.

Not all Fourth of July celebrations in Central Oregon started off with such a literal bang, but each and every one has been colorful. Many had unique features worth remembering.

Bend's Fourth of July celebration in 1904 was a big attraction. People from Madras, Post and Squaw Creek made the trip by wagon to camp along the river bank west of town. Townsfolk and visitors alike took part in the festivities which included a parade, horse races, bronco riding, barbeque and dancing with a caller. The baseball game rated front page coverage in the Bend *Bulletin*, coverage that reported nearly every play of the game. For parade watchers over the years, the parade route will sound familiar. Forming at the Pilot Butte Inn (corner of Greenwood and Wall), the parade progressed down Wall to Ohio (later renamed Franklin), over to Bond, and up Bond to Minnesota where a pavillion had been erected. A highlight of the day was the reading of the Declaration of Independence.

Prineville and other communities held their own celebrations in 1905, as the Fourth of July spirit was spreading throughout Central Oregon. But in 1907 Prineville was expected to come to Bend en masse to celebrate the 4th.

The big drawing card was the trout barbeque. For days ahead, teams brought in the day's catch well packed in ice. Each family brought a basket dinner to go along with the trout, which was free. Another big attraction was the baseball game, this year between Bend and Prineville High Schools. Men watered down the dusty streets for several days in advance of the celebration. The other well-advertised and unique feature of that year's celebration was free restrooms for the "ladies and little ones."

Throughout the early 1900's, an important event of any Fourth of July celebration was the reading of the Declaration of Independence or a speech by an orator, usually a prominent citizen of one of the towns

in Central Oregon. Every year or so a new event was presented. In 1912 it was hot air balloon ascensions. On July 6th of that year, Kit Carson's Buffalo Ranch Wild West Show came to town. In 1917, in addition to the usual parade and baseball game, Bend held a Big Water Festival in Drake Park. Canoe races, swimming races across the river, a greased pole contest, log rolling, canoe war, and goose chases highlighted the day.

The increasing popularity of automobiles influenced Bend's street events of the 4th in 1918. The crowd clustered along Oregon Street between Wall and Bond to see the "slow auto race around the block."

Fourth of July celebrations across our country in 1919 took on very special meanings. World War I, the Great War, had just ended with the signing of the peace treaty June 28th. In Bend, the Victory Celebration Parade Committee planned one of the biggest parades ever. The word went out that every automobile in the county, decorated or not, was wanted in the parade. Prizes were given for the Best Decorated Private Automobile (not a Ford) and for Best Decorated Ford.

In addition to the dynamite blasts of 1921, other events livened up the celebrations during the 20's. One of the largest attractions of all in 1922 was the Big Boxing Smoker. Boxing continued to be a drawing card into the 30's, with the 1934 program advertising 30 boxing events. If you were among the Fourth of July participants in Bend in 1923, you discovered that all places of business closed on the Fourth with the exception of those serving food or soft drinks. You also discovered that it was all too easy to be fined for some imagined "misdemeanor." But all to a good cause. Fine money went into the local Boy Scout Fund.

Indians from Warm Springs dressed in full regalia highlighted the 1924 parade led by the Shevlin-Hixon band. A Bend merchant, in the spirit of the Fourth, passed out free ice cream cones to all the Indians as the parade went through town. What a sight to behold on a hot sunny Fourth, Indian braves and warriors licking at dripping ice cream cones.

Along with sack races, tug-of-wars and water events in the 20's, a fat man's race was often featured. In 1930 the fat man's race became "a dash for corpulent men." And while Bend did, indeed, have a celebration that year, Central Oregon's biggest celebrations were held in Prineville and Silver Lake. Silver Lake's festivities included a special Bend Day. Bend's 30-piece band played concerts at the Silver Lake rodeo ground.

Then in 1933 a group of Bend American Legion members, many of them University of Oregon alumni who recalled with fond memories the canoe fetes on the Eugene Millrace and Pond, proposed the same general idea for a grand water pageant. Even though the Great Depression affected Bend just as anywhere else, the merchants of Bend rallied behind the chairman of the Water Pageant, B.A. "Dutch" Stover, and presented the biggest extravaganza ever. In addition to the usual rodeo, pet parade, street events, dances, boxing, and fireworks, this was the first year of Bend's Water Pageant.

Ten thousand people gathered in Drake Park to see the night time parade of floats glide along the river. Spotlights along the river and a full moon helped illuminate the floats as they were guided along by rowboats,

1959 Water Pageant Queen and her court. Photo by William L. Van Allen.

and, in some cases, swimmers. Patricia Neal was the first Queen Central Oregon. In subsequent years, the queen rode on a large swan float, and her court rode on smaller swan or cygnet floats. Another refinement of later pageants was the building of a boom in the river with walkways so that the floats could be pulled back up river.

The 1934 Water Pageant Queen, Lois Maker Gumpert, remembers the glorious years of the Water Pageants in a brief history written for the Deschutes Historical Center. She writes, "The success of the pageant was immediate. The first year the rodeo drew 5,000 spectators, and the Water Pageant had an estimated crowd of 10,000. By the mid-thirties hotels, motels and campgrounds were filled to capacity on July 4th weekend, and the newspapers were asking residents to open their homes to tourists."

Each Water Pageant showcased 16 to 20 floats that passed through a lighted arch that measured 48 feet high and 90 feet long. The opening had a clearance of over 26 feet high, an opening needed for many of the magnificent floats. In 1940, Portland, Eugene, and Lakeview all entered floats. A Eugene *Register-Guard*

editorial stated: "We believe Bend's show has greater possibilities in years to come than Pasadena's annual Tournament of Roses. No other city has such a setting for a water pageant."

World War II caused the suspension of the Water Pageants until 1947 when they came back into being and were as popular as ever. In addition to the pageants, special entertainment and performers made their appearances. Miss America of 1960, Lynda Lee Mead, was a headliner that year, a year that saw not one but three nights of the spectacular water pageant. And spectacular it was with the Fountain of Waters. Nineteen motors forced thousands of gallons of water into 4,000 jets to outdo any previous 4th of July display.

As mentioned earlier, the crowds converging on Bend for July Fourth celebrations grew larger than local motels, hotels and campgrounds could handle. The pageants of 1962-65 were separated from the Independence Day festivities and moved into late July. By the end of the '65 pageant, it was clear that crowds were unwieldy and that the financial burden was more than local merchants could continue to assume.

TOP: Sixteen to twenty Water Pageant floats would pass through the lighted arch on Mirror Pond in Drake Park (photo circa 1959). RIGHT: The arch measured 48 feet high and 90 feet long with a clearance of over 26 feet (photo circa 1962). BOTTOM: The pet parade through downtown Bend was an annual Fourth of July attraction for both young and old (photo circa 1960). Photos by William L. Van Allen.

Burnt Ranch:

*Where the present moves
in the shadow of the past . . .*

By Olive Colburn

Let us take a journey back through time, over the hills of an ancient land to those little old places our grandparents knew, back to that great and lonely land called "Eastern Oregon," especially Wheeler County.

Many who visit this country for the first time gaze out at this expanse of sand and sage and say "how desolate" and "this is a great place to be away from," and so they hurry through with never a backward glance. Others, who stop to look, see

A family gathering at the ranch during the early 1900's. Photo courtesy of Charley and Eunice Maxwell.

Burnt Ranch in 1901. Massive Byrd Rock looms in the background. Photo courtesy of Arthur Campbell.

beauty and tranquility, gazing at the softly rolling hills studded with sage, or the rugged ramparts of a rimrock lined horizon, and they find peace.

Looking at those beautiful rugged hills, it is comforting to know that folded away in that small canyon somewhere, one can find a crystal spring of clear, cool water. In the distance the sad little call of magella, the turtledove, can lull one's troubled mind, and a rustle in the brush may reveal a timid cottontail, all telling one that this so-called desolate land is teeming with life, beauty and adventure.

Settlers came and established homes, ranches, post offices and towns. Many were promising, many failed and passed into oblivion, some remain as ghost towns, some remain as names only, almost forgotten, but not quite, for the present must always move in the shadow of the past.

Burnt Ranch is a name considered synonymous with the early history of Central Oregon. Not only is it among the first continually inhabited sites, but it has a romantic history as well.

The ranch is tucked away in the painted hills, on the southern bank of the John Day River, at the western edge of Wheeler County, just 15 miles from the town of Mitchell.

The homestead, sheltered by massive Byrd Rock, lies on the south bank of the John Day river, beyond the red hills and Cactus Ridge, a wilderness, until recently overrun by wild horses.

The ranch buildings, now as then, are surrounded by rising hills, covered with bunch grass, sage and juniper.

It is told that roving bands of Cayuse and Warm Springs Indians included the site as a favorite camping ground before the pack trains to the Canyon City mines used it in the early 19th century.

James Clark homesteaded the spot, and at the advent of Henry Wheeler's Dalles-Canyon City stage line in May 1864, maintained for the line a stage station. Native hay grew in profusion, making the site ideal for furnishing winter fodder. Throughout the years the Burnt Ranch stop had a reputation for comfort and hospitality, and was the stopping place on the stage line route to the west.

Clark and his brother-in-law, George Masterson, forded the river on September 17th, 1866, to cut driftwood. Suddenly, coming out of the hills beyond the ranch, they spotted Indians. In an attempt to outrace the Indians to the house, where they had left their rifles, they hurried across the river. Seeing that the race was hopeless, they veered left and up Bridge Creek, with the Indians in hot pursuit. After a few miles of hard riding, Masterson's mount, which was a work horse, failed. Clark continued on for help, while Masterson entered the river, and swam down Bridge Creek, to a deep hole, covered with thick brush, where he hid.

The Indians chased Clark several miles, then returned to search for Masterson, but were unable to ferret him out, so they returned to the ranch, to sack and burn the buildings. They stole four horses belonging to Henry Wheeler, valued at $600.00, and oldtimers say the contents of feather mattresses covered the yard like new fallen snow.

A group of packers, stopping at the next ranch, eight miles away, returned with Clark to search for Masterson. They called for some time, before Masterson, suspicious of their friendliness, and badly chilled, crawled from his hiding place.

Clark's wife had left earlier to visit relatives in the Willamette Valley, thus escaping certain death.

One great satisfaction, however, came to Clark sometime later, while he was driving stage for C.W. Lockwood. Indians stole horses from Henry Maupin's corral, during Clark's overnight stop there. On his drive the next morning near Cross Hollows, he spotted the Indians; returning to Maupin's place, he and Maupin and the sole stage passenger, pursued the thieves. Maupin shot the leader, Chief Paulina in the thigh; then Clark, recognizing Paulina as the leader who had fired Burnt Ranch, shot and killed Paulina.

The Ranch was purchased by Elza Stephens around 1901. Elza was born in Oregon in 1869 and previously operated the Muddy Ranch, in Jefferson County, but wanted the Burnt Ranch, in order to go into the livestock business.

Elza married Mary Ellen Pentecost, from North Dakota. They built a 10-room house in the old growth of trees where the original buildings stood, and raised a large family there. The nearby river provided a precious source of water. Stephens and his brothers hand dug a system of irrigation ditches that created lush growth wherever they led, and provided good grazing land, and deep green alfalfa fields.

The soil was good, and the weather moderate. They raised a fine orchard, peaches, apricots, almonds, walnuts, most anything did well, when irrigated.

With the cattle, turkeys, and chickens, the ranch was totally self supporting. It became a very popular place, people came from as far away as Prineville, to buy fruit at harvest time, enjoy the hospitality, and swim in the river hole, at the base of Byrd Rock at the back of the house.

Elza's wife, Mary Stephens, ran the Burnt Ranch Post office out of a bedroom of the house, and that service proved to be a very important source of communication and transportation for the local ranchers, and homesteaders.

During the early 1900's Shaniko was still the main railroad shipping center in the Northwest. Wool, livestock, and anything else that needed to be shipped to markets from eastern Oregon, had to be driven by team into Shaniko. The Burnt Ranch was very important to the team drivers as an overnight campground spot as they travelled west.

Horses were fed and cared for, and often there was not enough money left to feed the drivers, so Mary would provide meals free.

Elza and Mary raised their large family on the ranch, and after they died, their son Tom Stephens purchased it. Tom, who is now 91 years old, and lives in nearby Mitchell, with his wife Eva, have lots of interesting stories about life on the ranch, which he purchased from the family, after his parents died in 1932.

"Old Tom" who seems just a part of this wild, colorful country, has spent all of his 91 years on and around the ranch. He met and married Eva Rickman who came to help his mother, and they are still enjoying married life together after more than 55 years.

He says that the best thing that ever happened to him — and the most excitement he ever had—was catching and breaking wild horses for fun and for profit.

Life was hard work, but it was real and it was good.

Tom and Eva had no sons. Their daughter Nelda, and husband Chuck Evans are operating the ranch, 9000 acres, on a limited capacity—so much hard work, but a healthy, happy life, and still the center for relatives and friends, to come and hash over the "good-old-days" once a year each July.

They say they have lots of company the entire year—friends, fishermen, hunters, and others who enjoy "them thar hills" in all the seasons.

Excerpts taken from: "The History of Wheeler Leaving Oregon" by permission of McClaren and Janet Stinchfield (Condon Times Journal)

TOP: Tom and Eva Stephens stand in front of the present day ranch house. Photo courtesy of the Stephens. BOTTOM: Tom and Eva were the Grand Marshalls at the 1987 Wheeler County Fair. Photo by Shirla Collins.

Little Known Tales
from Oregon History

No. 54

Cline Falls:
The Ghost That Vanished

By Don Burgderfer

The pickup eased to a stop at the end of the dirt road and I stepped out into the sage. The appearance of the area was no different than most other sage and juniper areas I had visited in Central Oregon - the same smells, the same quiet solitude (except for vague traffic noises in the distance) and the same sense of loneliness. But, I knew that this place was different, that it was a place of history whose physical evidence had largely vanished.

Where I was standing was once a bustling community. Like most pioneer communities, it was full of hope and plans and dreams for the future. But, in the end, there was ony oblivion except in the written chronicles and in the memories of the men and women who knew this place. And, today, most all of the living participants and physical remnants of the town of Cline Falls are gone.

Here I must make a small confession. I did not start to write anything about a pioneer *town* named Cline Falls. I had many times visited an attractive Deschutes River cascade named Cline Falls. It is about three miles west of Redmond on the highway to Sisters (State Highway 126). And it was the waterfall that mainly attracted my interest. In truth, I was led by the nose into the town of Cline Falls when I started to do some research on the origins of the hydroelectric facility which operates just below the falls.

My interest in the townsite was especially aroused by an interview that Frances Juris had with Cass Cline's daughter, Winifred Cline Jordan ("Old Crook County - The Heart of Oregon," by Frances Juris, Prineville Print Shop, 1975, p. 21). Winifred related how the Cline family settled in Central Oregon.

It was in September of 1887 that her dentist father, Dr. Cass A. Cline, his wife and two daughters, and his brother and his family crossed the Cascades into Central Oregon in search of homesteading land. They initially camped in ice caves south of what is now Bend because in those days there were no settlements in the area except Prineville. As winter turned harsh, the families moved farther north, eventually homesteading for awhile on the Metolius River.

When that particular area was taken over by the Warm Springs

Looking up Cline Falls toward the PP&L diversion dam. Photo by Don Burgderfer

Indian Reservation, Cass moved his family to Prineville and opened a dental office, becoming the first dentist in Central Oregon. But, he still had itchy feet, and later heard that homestead land was available on the Deschutes River. He moved the family to a site up on the west bank overlooking the beautiful waterfall on the Deschutes, probably around 1889 or 1890. Both the falls and the subsequent townsite became known as Cline Falls. Prominent buttes to the immediate southwest were named Cline Buttes in honor of the family.

But, Cass Cline was not to be a real part of the coming development of the town of Cline Falls. While living there, he did still maintain his dental practice in Prineville and "commuted" the twenty-three miles back and forth on a large bay stallion. Apparently, Mrs. Cline wasn't too happy about being so isolated at Cline Falls. They sold out to the recently formed Cline Falls Power and Irrigation Company and moved back to Prineville.

After several years in Prineville, the Clines moved to a homestead at Lower Bridge on the Deschutes and, after five years there, moved to

Redmond, where Dr. Cline practiced dentistry until he died in 1926. Winifred concluded her interview by observing that Cline Falls didn't even retain status as a ghost town because, unlike similar places, not a trace of it was left.

That nothing is left is somewhat surprising, considering the historical accounts of what *was* there: several stores, two hotels, a school, some fine homes (including Cline's), a livery stable, a stone jail and a newspaper publishing house. In 1904 the town was given approval for a post office!

The Cline Falls Power Company platted the town in 1904, subdividing 80 acres into 500 lots. To everyone's surprise, 60 lots were sold within the first three weeks, at prices from $60 to $250. A good account of the new town is given on page 732 in "An Illustrated History of Central Oregon," (Western Historical Publishing Company, Spokane, WA, 1905).

The Power Company seemed to have a lot going for it, and visionaries predicted great success for the area. At the turn of the century, the three key elements seemed imminent: good supplies of Deschutes River water to

irrigate the western benchlands of the river canyon, electrical power to be generated by the falls, and a railroad that was sure to pass through the townsite.

The founders of the Cline Falls Power Company had a right to their dreams. But Frank Redmond, three miles to the east, was a much better visionary! For it was to the future town of Redmond that the irrigation waters flowed, and it was through Redmond that the rails from Madras to Bend were laid. As for hydroelectric power generation, nothing occurred until late 1912, when a 75KW generator was brought in by George Jacobs, who had purchased Cline Falls Power and its water rights (rights which dated back to 1892). In 1930, interests associated with the Central Oregon Irrigation District bought the property, and they sold the power facilities to Pacific Power & Light in 1942.

In 1925, lightning destroyed the power house at Cline Falls. Then, in 1929, a fire destroyed the pumping plant. In 1943, with WWII raging, PP&L began construction of a new power plant, slightly downstream from the original one. It was

A view of the old and new Hwy. 126 bridges as seen from the ridge where the townsite of Cline Falls was located. Photo by Don Burgderfer

especially needed to help serve the needs of army and air force personnel stationed in the Redmond area. During WWII, troops with tanks even staged maneuvers in the immediate area of the old townsite and falls.

I spoke with Marion Henderson, PP&L's Bend Area Power Superintendant, about the present facility at Cline Falls. He said that the single turbine puts out 1100 kilowatts of power, or about 1475 horsepower. Also, he said that the elevation of the water at the top of the dam is 2827 feet and that the water drops 46 feet as it courses through the turbine. Marion did not indicate any particular plans by PP&L to enlarge or change the existing facilities in the near future.

To visit this scenic area, one need only drive about three miles west of the Redmond city limits on State Highway 126. For the best views of the falls and power house, I suggest that you turn right on SW 71st Street (at the top of the grade, before you go down and across the river) and wind down to the river. The pavement ends at the old highway bridge across the river. It was completed in 1913 and is now blocked to vehicles. There are some gravel roads that will take you a bit farther north along the river (this side of the river was once a huge gravel pit) and from this area one can obtain a fine view of the falls. Incidentally, these falls are simply spectacular during very cold winter weather because of the ice formations that build up.

A different view of the falls and power house can be had by going on across the river on the "new" highway bridge (completed in 1957), turning right on Eagle Drive and proceeding up a short grade on the paved road. If you should turn left on a dirt road at the top of this grade and follow it back south, you will be practically in the middle of what was once the city of Cline Falls! If you walk around a bit, you will see some old rotten boards on the ground, some rusty cans, even a bit of rusty barbed wire.

You might hope, as I did, that these are the last meager relics of the old townsite. Alas, informants such as Joyce Zobrist and Oma Sage assure me these things are of more recent origin. Even the old stone jail has vanished. Oma knows about these things - she grew up in the area, lives in Redmond, and helps run the Deschutes County Historical Society facility in Bend.

Joyce Zobrist knows about Cline Falls because she has lived in that immediate area for many years, and also works for the State Parks and Recreation Division of the Oregon Department of Transportation. I came into contact with Joyce when I called State Parks to get information on the Cline Falls State Park, which happens to be just on the other side of the bridge from the falls.

According to Joyce, the park area was first obtained by the state in 1936, had 2.75 acres added to it in 1956, and as of 1987 had a total of 9.04 acres. This is strictly a day-use facility for picnicing, fishing, wading and swimming. I guess I guffawed a bit when Joyce mentioned swimming, but she told me, "That's where I learned to swim!" Though the park is open round-the-clock in the summertime, overnight camping is not encouraged. Joyce said that the park area was originally acquired by the state in 1936 to be a gravel pit.

So, I started out to write a little piece about a scenic waterfall I had visited occasionally through the years. Instead, I learned a bit of interesting Central Oregon history. And I met some pretty interesting people in the process, both vicariously and in person. It became a trip through time and a quest for a vanished piece of our past.

I can stand at the old townsite now and know that it was not always just empty sage and juniper benchland. I can see Cass Cline starting off on another of those interminable 23 mile trips to Prineville to fix and pull teeth. I can hear the excited conversations in the stores about how the railroad will be coming this way any day now. And how soon will the life-giving irrigation water flow upon the benchland, as was promised? And that Frank Redmond over to the east - he must be crazy to set up a homestead in the middle of that desert! What is he thinking?

I can stand there and feel the defeat, the depths of disappointment in the awful realization that the rails won't come, the water won't flow, the main road will favor that crazy fellow three miles east, and this place will remain a desert. And Cline Falls died.

Through the years, I have stood in many western ghost towns and listened to the voice on the wind. The message is nearly always the same: "The lode has played out - it's time to git."

At the PP&L power plant, water is diverted from above the falls through the flume at the left side of the photo. Cline Falls townsite was just over the ridge behind the power plant. Photo by Don Burgderfer

Return of the BEND W·I·N·T·E·R

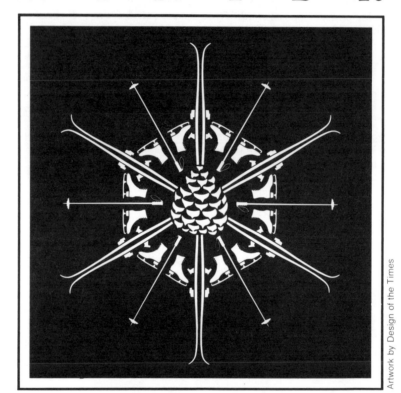

Artwork by Design of the Times

CARNIVAL

By Diane Kulpinski

Once upon a time in the land of Bachelor, there was an annual event called the Winter Carnival. Legend has it that the late February event created quite a festive atmosphere in the town of Bend. So festive in fact, that after only three years, the city decided to put an end to all the merrymaking.

Yes folks, it seems Bend has some rowdy history to it. Ask anyone who was around the area during the early 1960s about the old Winter Carnival and their immediate reaction will bring a warm smile to their face and a somewhat devilish chuckle from their lips.

Let's go back in time to when a cord of wood cost $15. The Bend *Bulletin*

was an average eight pages long and cost 10 cents. To a time when local telephone prefixes were listed as EV- for Evergreen, instead of 38-. Mt. Bachelor was then called Bachelor Butte and had only one chair lift and a couple of tow ropes. The population of Bend was hovering around the 12,000 mark. And just about everyone gave out S&H Green Stamps. Ah yes, back to the time when hootenannies were the fad of entertainment and kids had "chock-full-of-fun."

The whole thing started back in 1956 when Portland State College's ski club sponsored a weekend of intra-club races at Mount Hood. Surrounding the races were other activities such as the coronation of a Winter

Carnival Queen and Court, a dance and talent show.

It wasn't until 1961 that Central Oregon College—which back then consisted of an office and library located at the old Bend Senior High School and held classes Monday through Thursday—was invited to participate in the carnival. Apparently, the event was getting a bit too large for the facilities at Mount Hood. When Bachelor Butte installed their first chair lift for the '61/62 season, COC was asked to join in the event, event, thereby making Bend the host city of what was officially called the Portland State Intercollegiate Winter Carnival.

That first February close to 1,000

collegians hit town with the old Pilot Butte Inn housing carnival headquarters. The weekend was filled with activities, including ski races, a talent show, a queen's coronation and ball on Friday. Saturday started off with a pancake breakfast, followed by more skiing, go-kart races downtown, a spaghetti feed, a bonfire and noise parade and ended with another dance. Sunday's events featured the last of the ski races and final awards. It all sounds fun enough.

But, as John Bowerman, then a student at the University of Oregon recalls, "it was just wild. There was a lot of drinking and dancing up at the mountain and in town," he said. We'd party till 4 a.m., get a couple hours of sleep and then head up to the mountain," he added. Bowerman, now a rancher outside of Antelope, has plenty of other memories of the Winter Carnival, but would prefer they not be printed. He is not alone.

The following year, 1963, the Winter Carnival was again a big event for Bend, making front page news during the weekend. Attendance more than doubled that year as nearly 2,800 carnivalers from more than 30 colleges flocked to town. Kids started coming into town a week ahead of the event so as not to miss out on any of the action. The Pilot Butte Inn was again inundated by co-eds, as was the rest of town.

LeRoy Newport, business manager for the Redmond School District these days, was then captain of the COC Ski Club/Team. He and his three roommates, Doug Vincent, John Wenger and Ron Radabaugh were the original ski bums of Bachelor. They all lived in a rundown four unit apartment which they fixed up to look like a European ski hostel. Calling it "Der Berghof," they would rent out beds, army cots and floor space to college co-eds in town for the Winter Carnival. One year with no room to spare, they were resourceful enough to rent the bath tub for 50 cents a night!

Newport also remembers sitting in the COC library with Radabaugh one evening pondering over who would represent the college as their candidate for queen. Spying Micki Sickles, a student librarian who as Newport recalls "looked like a librarian and was very shy," they asked her to take off her "atrocious" glasses for them. She did and when they pulled her long hair back off her face they both agreed she was the one. Taking up a collection among their skiing friends, they managed to pay for her to get a haircut. Insisting that she not wear glasses during carnival weekend, she had to be led around during the festivities. But it was not in vain, as Sickles

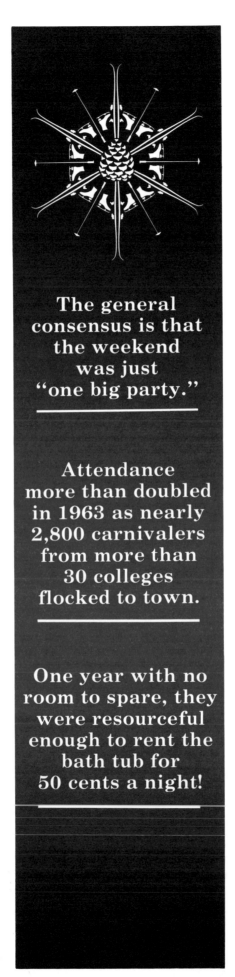

The general consensus is that the weekend was just "one big party."

Attendance more than doubled in 1963 as nearly 2,800 carnivalers from more than 30 colleges flocked to town.

One year with no room to spare, they were resourceful enough to rent the bath tub for 50 cents a night!

was crowned Winter Carnival Queen for 1963.

Central Oregon College's ski team also faired well that year as they took fourth place overall, led by Newport's second place in the Giant Slalom.

By 1964, the carnival had become one of THE events of the year, boasting itself as the largest intercollegiate ski event in the west. Forty-six colleges and universities from the Pacific Northwest, California, and Nevada drew close to 6,000 people into Bend that February. By this time a 40-meter ski jumping event, held at Skyliner's Hill near Tumalo Falls, had been added to the alpine and cross country event. Likewise, the fun-loving co-eds also increased the antics surrounding the weekend.

"Mooning" seemed to be a popular thing to do. Doug Vincent, a Redmond saddlemaker, recalls the U. of O. football team coming into town displaying their cheeks to everyone from the confines of their bus. Full moons could also be seen shining in the brilliant sunlight on the slopes. "Lusty ski ballads" and acts that just "escaped being risque" according to newspaper reports, seemed a big hit at the talent show that year.

As people remember it, kids would dance and party hop, drink in public and be just downright rowdy. The general consensus is that the weekend was just "one big party." One tale has it that a wall was torn down in order to make room for a party going on in the Pilot Butte Inn. Of course this has never been confirmed, but quite a few people seem to be familiar with the story.

Paul Reynolds, now a local funeral director, was mayor of Bend during that time. He, like most others who were around then, laughs now about all the shenanigans that went on. But 1964 would be the last year that Bend would host the event.

The Bend *Bulletin* reported in its Tuesday, Feb. 25, 1964 edition that "rumors of considerable weekend vandalism" had been modified. The front page article also said that "the majority of motel owners and others who had contact with the college guests" found that the group "as a whole, were 'very well behaved.'"

However, Reynolds said, there were quite a number of complaints lodged to city hall in connection with the weekend. He recalls the carnival as "just getting so big, it got out of hand. The community couldn't cope with it anymore. The city got scared, it (the city) wasn't big enough to handle the event." Therefore, future plans of holding the Winter Carnival in Bend were nixed.

Did You Miss Volume I?

Little Known Tales from Oregon History

Volume I

Send name, address and $12.00 (includes postage and handling) to:
Sun Publishing, P.O. Box 5784, Bend, OR 97708
or ask for it at your favorite book or gift shop.